GOD'S
REMARKABLE PLAN
FOR THE NATIONS

Darrow L. Miller | Bob Moffitt | Scott D. Allen

Disciple Nations Alliance

Founded by
Harvest and Food for
the Hungry International

YWAM Publishing is the publishing ministry of Youth With A Mission. Youth With A Mission (YWAM) is an international missionary organization of Christians from many denominations dedicated to presenting Jesus Christ to this generation. To this end, YWAM has focused its efforts in three main areas: (1) training and equipping believers for their part in fulfilling the Great Commission (Matthew 28:19), (2) personal evangelism, and (3) mercy ministry (medical and relief work).

For a free catalog of books and materials, contact:

YWAM Publishing
P.O. Box 55787, Seattle, WA 98155
(425) 771-1153 or (800) 922-2143
www.ywampublishing.com

God's Remarkable Plan for the Nations
Copyright © 2005 by Darrow L. Miller, Bob Moffitt, and Scott D. Allen

10 09 08 07 06 05   10 9 8 7 6 5 4 3 2 1

Published by Youth With A Mission Publishing
P.O. Box 55787
Seattle, WA 98155

ISBN 1-57658-352-X

Printed in the United States of America.

Kingdom Lifestyle Bible Studies

God's Remarkable Plan for the Nations
God's Unshakable Kingdom
The Worldview of the Kingdom of God

Acknowledgments

This project has truly been a team effort. Many thanks to Randy Hoag, President of Food for the Hungry International, for his vision to develop this series and for his encouragement along the way. Grateful thanks to Max Rondoni for his invaluable assistance in helping us organize a great mass of written materials and lecture notes into something we could work with. A debt of gratitude goes to Cindy Benn and Natalie Clarke for their help with editing and proofreading. We also gratefully acknowledge the expert editorial assistance of Judith Couchman. Not only did she bring a degree of professionalism to the writing of these lessons, she brought her heart and encouragement as well. Several others have contributed valuable insights in shaping the content of these lessons. Among these are Karla Tesch, David Conner, Dave Evans, Rhonda McEwen, Arturo Cuba, and Gary Zander. We also thank Warren Walsh, Marit Newton, Richard Kim, Janice Manuel, and all the other professionals at YWAM Publishing for the considerable time and energy they put into the development of these books. What an honor and privilege it has been to work with such a wonderful team of committed brothers and sisters in Christ.

Contents

⌒ Foreword

Greetings from a fellow pilgrim! I am so pleased that you are beginning this Bible study. My passion is to see people growing in their relationships with King Jesus and his kingdom. I pray that this book and learning process will be such a blessing to you.

This Kingdom Lifestyle series is based on the analogy of a tree. The Bible often uses the metaphor of a tree to describe the Christian life. For example, in Romans 11:16 we read, "If the part of the dough offered as firstfruits is holy, then the whole batch is holy; if the root is holy, so are the branches." So it is with our lives. To have abundant fruit, we need a strong trunk. To have a strong trunk, we need good roots. And all of that is dependent on rich soil. Like many profound truths, this concept is actually quite simple.

I am not only excited about the rich content of this series; I am also excited about the method. I am convinced that people learn best in small groups and by putting what they learn into practice. We were not created to grow alone.

This particular study, *God's Remarkable Plan for the Nations*, is about the big picture of God's plan of redemption. On a micro scale, we are concerned with our families, communities, and personal growth. If you put together all these communities and people, however, you have a nation. Nations are more than just collections of communities—distinct cultures and identities are created. Discipling nations, therefore, involves the transformation of individuals, communities, and entire cultures. The purpose of this book is to show you God's plan for and perspective on the nations, to renew your appreciation for the nations, and to expand your vision in discipling the nations.

May grace and joy abound in your life.

Serving the King and the kingdom together,
—Randy Hoag
President, Food for the Hungry International

About This Study

In this study, you'll learn about God's redemptive plan, how it has developed, and how you can participate in it. You can study by yourself or with a small group. There are six sessions in this study.

Theme of Each Session

Session 1. God raised up the nations. He has a heart for the nations and a plan to redeem them.

Session 2. In the Old Testament, God unfolded his redemptive plan through Israel.

Session 3. Jesus stands at the center of God's redemptive plan.

Session 4. God works through the worldwide church to unfold his redemptive plan.

Session 5. At the end of time, God's plan will be complete and his promise to bless all nations will be fulfilled.

Session 6. The global vision implied in the Great Commission (Matt. 28:18–20) is for all nations to be redeemed and restored, with their cultures reflecting God's kingdom.

Sections of Each Session

Key Words to Know. After the opening narrative, each session includes discussion of some of the key words found in the session. In addition to reading the provided definitions, you may wish to use additional resources, such as a Bible dictionary or commentary, for further study of these terms. Understanding these words will help you get the most out of the study.

Key Verses to Read. After the discussion of key words, you'll find a key Scripture passage for the session. Carefully read the quotation and answer the questions after it. These key verses provide a biblical framework for the central teaching of each session. Whether you're leading or participating in a small group or studying alone, you can consult the suggested responses for each session's Key Verses to Read questions in the Study Notes at the end of the book. Not all questions have a "right" or "wrong" answer, but these suggestions will help stimulate your thinking.

Biblical Insights. This narrative section is the heart of each session. Carefully read it, taking notes as you go along. As you read, highlight meaningful or important points and write down questions that come to mind.

Discovery Questions. This section is designed to take you into God's Word for a deeper understanding of the material covered in the Biblical Insights section. Suggested responses to these questions can be found in the Study Notes at the back of the book.

Key Points to Remember. This section briefly summarizes the key points for each session.

Closing Thoughts. This section provides a wrap-up of the session, designed to transition from the main body of the session to the personal application that follows.

Personal Application. Here's where the study gets personal. These questions are designed to help you reflect on your own life and experiences and move you toward personal application.

A Practical Response. The optional activities suggested at the end of the session will help you tangibly apply the biblical teachings presented in that lesson.

If you're leading a small group through this study, before beginning please read the Leader's Guide. Guidelines are provided that will help you enhance your group's effectiveness.

Please join us as we delve into Scripture and discover God's plan to bless, heal, and redeem the nations. This is a plan that touches your life profoundly, and God wants you to participate in it. What role will you play? How will he use you to influence others? How will this plan shape the story of your life? The answers could be exciting.

An Urgent Invitation to Reach the Nations

Often it's reassuring—and sometimes it's unsettling— when a person or group extends a promise to us. We're comforted that someone cares enough to pledge a longed-for action, but at the same time we might wonder if the promise will hold. In a promise, there's potential for delight or disappointment.

We can feel the same way about God. Will he keep his promises to us, to his children, to the world? The Bible says yes. King David wrote, "Your kingdom is an everlasting kingdom, and your dominion endures through all generations. The LORD is faithful to all his promises and loving toward all he has made" (Ps. 145:13). Centuries later the apostle Paul claimed, "For no matter how many promises God has made, they are 'Yes' in Christ" (2 Cor. 1:20). Whether or not some of God's promises have been fulfilled, or whether or not we're waiting for others to materialize, he stands unshakably by his commitment. We can dare to believe that God's promises will come true.

Four thousand years ago Abraham, the father of the nation of Israel and the forefather of the church, needed to decide whether he'd trust God's promises. The Lord pledged that all peoples of the earth would be blessed through Abraham and his offspring (Gen. 12:1–3). That was a huge promise, one that Abraham couldn't live long enough to see completely fulfilled. Yet true to his word, God has brought hope and healing to countless nations through Abraham and, specifically, through his most famous descendent, Jesus Christ.

Still a Broken World

Though much good has emerged through the centuries, we still live in a broken and hurting world. Evil, hunger, poverty, injustice, corruption, and enslavement mark the nations. Wars and ethnic tension plague many peoples. So while we've progressed in some areas, the improvements aren't enough. Every day approximately twenty-four thousand people die of hunger or hunger-related diseases, and three-fourths of them are children.[1] Millions of people live in hopelessness and despair, never hearing the good news about Jesus Christ and the forgiveness of sins, never knowing about God's deep love for them and his desire to bless their nations. Increasingly, the poorest people of the world are the least evangelized. There is still much work to do.

Yet the Bible promises that God has a plan—a big agenda—to bless, heal, and redeem the nations of this world. God created the nations. He loves them and longs to bless them. There are more than two thousand references to "nations" in Scripture, and many concern God's desire to bless and heal them. In fact, he loves *your* nation and longs to bless it. More than that, he's promised he will! The history of every nation in the world has been—or will be—dramatically impacted by God's glorious redemptive plan.

God's redemptive plan is the central theme of the *entire* Bible. It's the common thread that unites the Old and New Testaments. It's a plan that begins immediately after Adam and Eve's separation from God in Genesis chapter 3 and doesn't conclude until the final chapters of Revelation. Why did God make his covenant with Abraham? Why did he create and bless the nation of Israel? Why did he send his Son, Jesus, to die on the cross? Why did he raise up the worldwide church? What does he want to accomplish through this church in our generation? For the answer to each of these questions, we need to understand something of God's big agenda—his history-encompassing redemptive plan for the nations.

To appreciate the scope of this remarkable plan, it's important to study more than passages or even a book in the Bible. Instead we must look at the Scriptures as a complete, unified whole. We need to capture a bird's-eye view of the Bible and attempt to understand its "big picture." The Bible's unified theme is a miracle in itself. It isn't a single book but a library of sixty-six individual books, written by many different authors from varying cultural backgrounds over more than two thousand years. And yet God amazingly wove each of these diverse strands together into a beautiful tapestry that reveals his plan to heal, bless, and redeem the nations.

More Than Individuals

But why is a nation important? Isn't it just a collection of people who share a common language and geographic location? Isn't God's redemptive plan focused primarily on individuals? While it's true that God's redemption begins with individuals, it's more comprehensive—more wonderful—than this. God's plan advances around the world as individuals hear and accept the gospel by faith, are spiritually born again (John 3:3), and experience inward regeneration. Yet it also encompasses the healing and transformation of entire nations and cultures.

Of course, nations are made up of people, but in a certain sense they're greater than the sum of their parts. Every nation has a personality or character of its own, with its unique customs, attitudes, and history. Nations also share many common "spheres" that determine how each functions. These spheres include law, commerce, education, and government. God's redemptive interest covers all of these aspects of nations as well. His redemption moves forward as Christians and churches understand the fullness of this plan and bless the nations by sharing and living out biblical truth in <u>every</u> part of society. This is a critical point that many Christians overlook, including many in today's missionary community.

Ultimately, will the church in our generation be faithful to Jesus' command to make disciples of all nations according to the fullness of what he intended? Will the blessings of God—promised to Abraham four thousand years ago—be extended to contemporary nations? For this to occur, we must regain a comprehensive understanding of God's remarkable plan for the nations. These are the issues and questions we pose in this Bible study, encouraging you to consider them for yourself and your local church.

—Scott D. Allen

God's Remarkable Plan for the Nations

Many of us live in cultures that honor fame. We often hear about celebrities who are rich, talented, or leaders in some way. Sometimes even evil or simply eccentric or humorous people become famous. But one of the most significant people of all time was a nomadic herdsman who only wanted to keep his flocks and family together in a harsh desert climate.

That man was Abraham, whose story unfolds in the book of Genesis. It's impossible to overestimate his importance to world history. Three contemporary world religions—Judaism, Islam, and Christianity—trace their roots back to him. He's a central character throughout Scripture, and modern historians claim we know more about him than about any other person who lived four thousand years ago.

If we're familiar with the Old Testament, this shouldn't surprise us. Abraham's name is great because God made a covenant with him. It's a promise that touches every nation on earth. Through a covenant with Abraham, God revealed his plan for the world and how it would be fulfilled. Through this promise, we can catch a glimpse of God's heart for the nations.

In this lesson you'll learn about God's redemptive plan, that is, the nature of his promise and how it has unfolded through the centuries. Then you will consider how to participate in this exciting, world-changing venture.

KEY WORDS TO KNOW
What's in a Nation?

Nation

In the Old Testament, the primary usage for *nation* is the Hebrew word *mishpachah*, which means a family group, tribe, or clan. The New Testament uses the Greek word *ethnos*, indicating a race, people, or ethnic group. Some Bible translations, such as the New International Version, substitute the word "peoples" for nations, but the root word is the same. While reading the Bible, it's important not to confuse the modern meaning for the word *nation*, which is a nation-state, with the biblical use of the word. For example, Ethiopia is a nation-state, but it is home to nearly one hundred people groups or nations (in the biblical sense).

Redeem (Redemption/Redemptive)

To redeem means to save or rescue someone or something or to liberate someone from captivity or bondage. Biblically, the word *redeem* often refers to the rescue and deliverance of a person or people from the bondage of sin and the penalties for the violation of God's laws.

Covenant

In the Bible, the word *covenant* represents a solemn agreement that binds parties to each other in a permanent, defined relationship. The agreement includes promises, claims, and responsibilities for everyone involved. When God makes a covenant in Scripture, he alone establishes the terms. In the Old Testament, the basic covenant between God and the nation of Israel is "I will take you as my own people, and I will be your God" (Exod. 6:7). The responsibility for Israel is to "love the LORD your God and keep his requirements, his decrees, his laws and his commands always" (Deut. 11:1).

KEY VERSES TO READ

A Journey and a Blessing

The LORD had said to [Abraham], "Leave your country, your people and your father's household and go to the land I will show you.

"I will make you into a great nation
    and I will bless you;
I will make your name great,
    and you will be a blessing.
I will bless those who bless you,
    and whoever curses you, I will curse;
and all peoples [nations] on earth
    will be blessed through you."

—*Genesis 12:1–3* [2]

1. What three things did God ask Abraham to leave behind?

   _____

   _____

2. Where did God ask Abraham to go?

   _____

   _____

3. List the six "I will" statements that God promised to Abraham.

   _____

   _____

   _____

   _____

4. If Abraham obeyed, what would be the end result of God's covenant with him?

   _____

   _____

5. What is God's plan for every nation through Abraham?

_____

_____

BIBLICAL INSIGHTS
It's in Our Blood

Did you know that we're all related to one another? It's an intriguing thought for historians and family-tree buffs. The Bible clearly states that all peoples, races, and cultures carry the same blood in their veins (Acts 17:26). The lineage of each nation and individual ultimately traces back to the first couple, Adam and Eve. Genesis 3:20 says, "Adam named his wife Eve, because she would become the mother of all the living." She is the mother of the human race. Today thousands of nations inhabit the world, yet each one connects to the others. They all descend from the same blood.

Just as God blessed Adam and Eve, he intends to bless the world's nations. But unfortunately, because of this first couple's rebellion against God, the nations live with brokenness, poverty, conflict, and sorrow. The original source of this misery is found in Genesis 3, where it tells of the first couple turning their backs on the Creator. As the apostle Paul described it, "Sin entered the world through one man [Adam], and death through sin, and in this way death came to all men, because all sinned" (Rom. 5:12).

This first act of disobedience toward God by his created image-bearers is known as the Fall. This original sin not only separated the couple from God but negatively affected every part of his created order (Rom. 8:18–25). It affected humanity's relationship with God. It affected people's relationships with one another and humanity's relationship with the rest of creation. It even affected each person's relationship with him- or herself. Nothing was left untouched. The results of this downfall are plain to see, not only in the pain, conflict, and suffering around us but in our own lives too.

The good news is that God didn't abandon his creation in this fallen condition. He immediately began to reveal his plan to redeem, restore, and heal everything broken by sin. The history of every nation belongs to this redemptive plan for the world.

After the Fatal Fall

After the biblical accounts of the Fall and the worldwide flood in Genesis 1–9, the Lord repopulated the earth through one family, Noah and his descendants (Gen. 10). The next chapter tells the pivotal story of the Tower of Babel and the birth of the world's nations.

> Now the whole world had one language and a common speech. As men moved eastward, they found a plain in Shinar and settled there.
>
> They said to each other…, "Come, let us build our-selves a city, with a tower that reaches to the heavens, so that we may make a name for ourselves…."
>
> But the LORD came down to see the city and the tower that the men were building. The LORD said, "If as one people speaking the same language they have begun to do this, then nothing they plan to do will be impossi-ble for them. Come, let us go down and confuse their language so they will not understand each other."
>
> So the LORD scattered them from there over all the earth.
>
> —Genesis 11:1–8

Why is the story of Babel a pivotal moment in Scripture? Before Babel humanity consisted of one language and culture group. At Babel, God confused the people's language and scattered them over the face of the earth. Multiple nations were born. In creating the nations, God set the stage for his redemptive agenda—a plan he would unfold through indi-vidual people and nations from that point forward.

The First Biblical Appearance

Immediately after the account of Babel, Abraham appears for the first time in Scripture. He was a man from one of the many new nations. As noted in the earlier section, Key Verses to Read, God's covenant with Abraham presents the clearest revelation of his redemptive plan and purpose thus far in Scripture. In this covenant, God promised Abraham three things: (1) I will make you into a great nation, (2) I will make your name great, and (3) I will bless you. At the Tower of Babel, the builders wanted to make a name for themselves. In contrast, God called Abraham into a special relationship with his Creator and promised to make this nomad's name great. But why did God promise these gifts to Abraham? God revealed the answer by giving him a responsibility: "All peoples on earth will be blessed through you" (Gen. 12:3).

In one short sentence, God revealed his magnificent plan for the world's redemption, healing, and restoration. God chose Abraham and blessed him for a purpose: that he would be a blessing to others, and by the end of the age, every nation would be blessed. While God demonstrated his love to Abraham through this promise, it's clear that his love extended to the entire world. God's covenant revealed his compassionate heart for the nations.

But how were "all peoples on earth" to be blessed through Abraham? What did God mean when he offered this strange promise and affirmed it again and again (see Gen. 18:18; 22:18; 26:4; 28:14)? The full impact of this promise would not be understood for another two thousand years. At the God-appointed time, the most famous of Abraham's descendants, Jesus Christ, would die on a cross to extend blessings to people from every nation.

God chose to unfold his plan through *one man*. In fact, throughout Scripture God has carried out his plan through individuals. Some were well known, like Moses, Deborah, Esther, David, and Paul. Others were lesser known, like Rahab, Stephen, and Dorcas. Yet each played a vital part in unfolding God's redemptive plan. Their stories underscore that God uses individual men and women to carry out his plan. As a result, every human life has astounding eternal significance.

DISCOVERY QUESTIONS
A Closer Look at God's Plan

The great significance of the nations—and of the individuals who belong to them—holds even more meaning when you study the Scriptures yourself. Open your Bible to read more about God's plan for the nations and for you.

1. Read Acts 17:26–27 and answer the following questions.

    a. Describe God's sovereign control over the nations, stated in verse 26.

    _____

    _____

    b. Based on this short passage, what is God's desire for the nations?

    _____

    _____

    c. What does this passage and Genesis 3:20 affirm about all peoples, races, and cultures?

    _____

    _____

2. Read Hebrews 6:13–17 to answer the next questions.

    a. Why did God make a promise and also swear an oath?

    _____

    _____

    b. As best you can tell, what did the oath accomplish?

    _____

    _____

c.   What are the effects of this oath on every nation?

_____

_____

3.   Read the following passages. What do they reveal about God's covenant with Abraham?

Psalm 117

_____

_____

Romans 15:7–13

_____

_____

Revelation 7:9–10

_____

_____

4.   How could God's covenant affect your nation?

_____

_____

_____

KEY POINTS TO REMEMBER
The Nations in Review

1.   God created and loves each nation.
2.   Because Adam and Eve rebelled against God, all nations are plagued by brokenness, conflict, and sorrow (Rom. 5:12).
3.   God has a plan for redeeming individuals and nations from the bondage of sin and the destructive effects of the Fall (Col. 1:19–20).
4.   Through a covenant, God promised to make Abraham's descendants into a great nation that blesses all nations.

5. God carries out his redemptive plan through individuals. This means every person has astounding, eternal significance.

CLOSING THOUGHTS
Praise for God's Plan

God reveals himself in the Bible as the "compassionate and gracious God" (Exod. 34:6–7). Out of his great love for creation, he launched a history-encompassing plan for redeeming the world. You're part of that world, and God wants to redeem you and your nation.

Praise God that he loves you and redeems you from sin. Praise him that he loves your nation and longs to bless and heal it. Praise him that your life has great significance. Ask God how he wants to use you in his remarkable redemptive strategy.

PERSONAL APPLICATION
What About Your Nation?

God deeply loves and wants to redeem every nation. Use these insights and questions to apply this session's principles to your nation and to think about your part in God's redemptive plan.

1. God created everyone and everything. So each nation, though marked by sin and destruction, still reflects his glory and blessing. No matter how spiritually or physically broken your nation may be, its people, culture, heritage, and structure harbor positive characteristics. Think about what's great about your nation. What do you like about its outlook, people, customs, or other aspects of its culture? List three to five of these positive attributes below.

_____

_____

_____

_____

_____

2. From the list you just created, which characteristic do you like best about your nation? Why? How does this characteristic affect you personally?

_____

_____

_____

3. Now reflect on the spiritual nature of your nation. What is your nation's relationship to God? Describe it in a few sentences.

_____

_____

_____

_____

4. How does your nation's spiritual outlook affect you and/or your life?

_____

_____

_____

_____

5. Because of sin's influence, every nation also experiences brokenness. What are the most significant areas of brokenness in your nation? List at least three.

_____

_____

6. Which of these areas of brokenness concerns you the most? Why? How does it affect you personally?

_____

_____

_____

_____

7. Currently, are you doing anything to bring redemption to this area of brokenness? If so, what? If not, are you ready to begin? Why, or why not?

_____

_____

_____

_____

A PRACTICAL RESPONSE
Blessings and Brokenness

Try these optional activities to better target and understand your nation's character and to pinpoint and pray for its needs.

Make a Map

Obtain or draw a rough map of your country or nation. On the left side of the map, create a list titled "Blessings." Under this heading, list the blessings God has bestowed on your nation. For example, the list could contain items like freedom, artistic nature, social consciousness, strong sense of heritage, etc. Consult answers from question 1 in the Personal Application section to make the list. If you're part of a group, choose together which of your many answers belong on the map.

To the right of the map, write the title "Brokenness" and list the wounded aspects of your nation and its people. The list could include things like cults, drugs, poverty, oppression of minorities and women, etc. Consult answers from question 5 in the Personal Application section to create your list.

Place the map on a wall so you or your study group can see it during each session. Use the map as a reminder to apply this study's truths to your nation and to pray for its needs and your part in meeting them.

You could also draw a line or run a string from each characteristic to the major area it affects in your nation. For example, if illegal drugs persist in a predominant area of your nation, create a line from "drugs" to that area.

Plan to Pray

Based on the map made in the first activity (or lists you create on note-paper), develop a prayer plan for your nation. Fill in the chart below, dividing your nation's blessings and brokenness into six prayer sessions. At the end of each study session, take a few moments to thank God for the blessings and to intercede for the brokenness.

Also ask God how you could participate in healing the brokenness. Jot down anything that comes to mind.

	Blessings	**Brokenness**
Session 1 Date:		
Session 2 Date:		
Session 3 Date:		
Session 4 Date:		
Session 5 Date:		
Session 6 Date:		

The next session: *God's redemptive work through the nation of Israel*

Israel's Important Role in God's Plan

Most parents try not to "play favorites," wanting to love and treat their children equally. Employers also benefit from fair and equal treatment of their employees. Even if we live under a government that represses its people, we carry a sense of injustice when leaders favor some groups over others. Consequently, with our twenty-first-century mind-set, God's selection of a "chosen people" might seem unfair.

Why would God narrow his attention to one nation as his favorite? Nearly the entire Old Testament encompasses a history of God's relationship with Abraham's blood offspring, the nation of Israel. By contrast, the New Testament is more international, focusing on preaching the good news about Jesus around the world. Despite this surface appearance, God's love for all nations was as true in the Old Testament as it is today. From Genesis chapter 12 forward, his plan of global redemption has pivoted on raising up and blessing a chosen nation to serve as a channel of blessing to all other nations. In the Old Testament, that nation was Israel. In the New Testament, that nation is the church. The connection between the Old and New Testaments, and between the nation of Israel and the church, is deep and profound. That's why it's important to consider how Israel figures into God's redemptive agenda.

In this session you'll learn how God worked through Abraham's offspring, the nation of Israel, to carry out the first stage of this plan.

KEY WORDS TO KNOW

The Blessing of the Jews

Israel/the Jews

The word *Israel* is the new name given by God to Jacob, the son of Isaac and grandson of Abraham, after Jacob's famous wrestling match with God in Genesis 32:22–32. In fact, *Israel* means "to struggle with God." Later in the Old Testament, Israel became the common name for all of Jacob's descendants.

Jacob had twelve children, and their descendants became known as the twelve tribes of Israel, the children of Israel, or simply, the Israelites. When the kingdom of Israel divided at the death of King Solomon, the Northern ten tribes took the name *Israel* for themselves. The Southern Kingdom became known as Judah, which had been the name of the tribe that had become dominant in that region. After the Exile, the term *Israel* was once again applied to the whole people.

The word *Jew* was originally a term used by foreigners in the Hellenistic (or Roman) world. It comes from the Greek and Latin words for Judah, and the people thereof. The people of Israel didn't begin to use the term commonly to refer to themselves before the middle of the first century, when many (and finally, most) were scattered to places outside Palestine.

Today *Israel* describes both a nation-state and an ethnic group, and a Jew is someone with this ethnicity, even if he or she is a citizen of a nation-state other than Israel.

Blessing

In biblical times, the concept of *blessing* had a deep and profound meaning. To bless someone was to declare favor and goodness upon them. But it wasn't merely a wish for someone's happiness, or a polite thing to say; rather, it held the spiritual power to come true.

A blessing in the Old Testament often described a material or spiritual gift given by God to his people. God blessed people with life, wealth, fruitfulness, or abundance, even those who didn't seem to deserve it. In the New Testament, a blessing usually referred to a spiritual gift. God's greatest blessing, Jesus, erased our sins (Rom. 4:7–8) and promised eternal life.

Holy (holiness)

The word *holy* describes something that is whole or perfect in a moral sense. The Bible describes God as holy. He is pure and complete in moral character. *Holiness* also means "separation," and the term *holy* describes persons or things that have been separated or set apart for God and his service.

KEY VERSES TO READ
A King Seeks God's Favor

May God be gracious to us and bless us
　　and make his face shine upon us,
that your ways may be known on earth,
　　your salvation among all nations.
May the peoples praise you, O God;
　　may all the peoples praise you.
May the nations be glad and sing for joy,
　　for you rule the peoples justly
　　and guide the nations of the earth.
May the peoples praise you, O God;
　　may all the peoples praise you.
Then the land will yield its harvest,
　　and God, our God, will bless us.
God will bless us,
　　and all the ends of the earth will fear him.

—*Psalm 67*

1. David, the king of Israel, wrote Psalm 67. Why did this ruler seek God's blessing?

   _____

   _____

2. What does this passage reveal about God's intentions for the nations?

   _____

   _____

   _____

3. How is God's role described?

   _____

   _____

4. What will be the result of the nations' praising God?

   _____

   _____

5. What are the similarities between this psalm, written approximately one thousand years after God's covenant to Abraham, and Genesis 12:1–3?

   _____

   _____

   _____

BIBLICAL INSIGHTS
A Model and Messenger for the Kingdom

Within a few short generations of God's marvelous covenant with Abraham, his descendants suffered in bondage to Egypt. Far from being blessed, the children of Israel existed as a poor slave nation. For 430 years it was a nation of refugees acquainted only with pain, servitude, and cruel labor. Had God abandoned his promise to bless Abraham's offspring? Were they no longer the chosen ones?

While it may seem so, God was working behind the scenes, preparing Israel for its release from slavery—a rescue so miraculous that only God could pull it off. There was no Israelite army to confront the powerful Egyptians; they simply walked free, following behind Moses, their God-appointed leader. When the Egyptian army finally pursued them, God arranged a spectacular escape through the parted waters of the Red Sea (Exod. 13:17–14:31). The watching nations of the world couldn't help but be in awe of God's sovereign plan.

In God's sovereign plan, this poor, broken nation was released from bondage to become a model nation for the world—a chosen people, uniquely blessed by God. Yet God didn't show favor to Israel because it was the largest, strongest, or holiest nation on earth. (The Israelites repeatedly blundered in their relationship with God and needed his forgiveness.) He redeemed it because of his love for all nations and the binding covenant with Abraham to bless all nations through his offspring.

Through Moses, God reaffirmed his covenant with Israel. He promised to be Israel's God, and they would be his chosen people (Exod. 6:7). He also provided specific instructions about living to please him (20:1–17). The Lord instructed Israel that it would experience life, freedom, and prosperity by obeying his revealed laws, commands, and intentions. However, rejecting God's laws would earn death and destruction. God's covenant with Israel hinged on the condition of obedience.

A Treasured Possession

When God reiterated his covenant of blessing in Exodus 19, he said that if Israel obeyed his commands, it would enjoy a unique status among the nations. He explained, "Now if you obey me fully and keep my covenant, then out of all nations you will be my treasured possession. Although the whole earth is mine, you will be for me a kingdom of priests and a holy nation" (Exod. 19:5–6). Israel would be God's treasured possession. What a blessing! What an honor!

Lest the Israelites feel haughty or superior, God also quickly reminded them of this blessing's purpose. "The whole earth is mine!" proclaimed the Lord. "My love extends to *all* nations. Your duty is to be a kingdom of priests and a holy nation." In other words, Israel was to be a model nation—a holy nation—before the watching eyes of the world. Israel was also to be a messenger to the nations—a kingdom of priests—proclaiming the reality, nature, and character of the living God. Priests serve as intermediaries, as bridges between God and humans. This priestly role was Israel's responsibility in the world.

God revealed himself in a special way to his chosen people. They in turn served as a witness to the reality of God before the watching eyes of the world. The watching nations would stand in awe of his power and might, revealed through the nation's dramatic rescue from Egyptian enslavement. The watching nations would understand that God's laws are beneficial for creating free, just, and compassionate societies (Deut. 4:5–8; 28:1–14). Thus Israel had been blessed for a purpose. It was blessed to be a blessing.

May God Be Gracious

David, the great king of Israel, clearly understood God's plan to bless all nations and Israel's unique role in that plan. He profoundly and beautifully wrote about it in Psalm 67, the key passage for this session. "May God be gracious to us and bless us," wrote King David (vs. 1)—not so that Israel could enjoy God's blessing exclusively but so that God's "ways may be known on earth, your salvation among all nations" (vs. 2). This psalm, like Exodus 19:5–6 and Genesis 12:1–3, is part of the redemptive theme threaded throughout the Bible. God's plan for the world's redemption pivoted on raising up and blessing a chosen nation to serve as a channel of blessing to other nations.

But did other nations actually acknowledge and honor God as a result of Israel's example? A clear case occurs in 2 Chronicles when the leader of a foreign nation, the Queen of Sheba, visits King Solomon and tours the grand temple in Jerusalem. Solomon was the son of King David who ascended the throne after David's death.

> When the queen of Sheba saw the wisdom of Solomon, as
> well as the palace he had built, ... she was overwhelmed.

She said to the king, "The report I heard in my own
country about your achievements and your wisdom is
true. But I did not believe what they said until I came
and saw with my own eyes. Indeed, not even half the
greatness of your wisdom was told me; you have far
exceeded the report I heard.... Praise be to the LORD
your God, who has delighted in you and placed you on
his throne as king to rule for the LORD your God. Because
of the love of your God for Israel and his desire to uphold
them forever, he has made you king over them, to main-
tain justice and righteousness."

—2 Chronicles 9:3–8

As promised, God's blessing extended to other nations through Israel.
In fact, in this instance, Solomon had prayed to God, specifically asking
him to bless foreign nations through the newly completed temple (2 Chron.
6:32–33). God answered the king's request.

The Gifts of the Jews

Beautiful temples and abundant living weren't all that Israel contributed to the world. Its influence permeated cultures throughout history.
Historian Thomas Cahill described the impact of Israel on the nations of
the world in his book *The Gifts of the Jews*:

We can hardly get up in the morning or cross the street
without being [affected by thoughts and ideas that came
to us through the nation of Israel]. We dream Jewish
dreams and hope Jewish hopes. Most of our best words,
in fact—*new, adventure, surprise; unique, individual, person, vocation; time, history, future; freedom, progress, spirit;
faith, hope, justice*—are the gifts of the Jews.[3]

Yes, many blessings were dispersed to the nations through God's chosen nation, Israel. Consider a few of the concepts that Cahill listed: *history*,

future, progress. Before Abraham, nations were trapped within a circular concept of time—an endless cycle of birth, life, and death; of spring, summer, fall, and winter; of planting, cultivating, and harvesting. History was going nowhere. Individual life felt meaningless. It seemed to have no purpose beyond simple survival. Fatalistic thinking was the norm. There was no hope for tomorrow, only the stark reality of today and yesterday. Yet, through the nation of Israel, God introduced humans to seldom-considered concepts such as history, future, and progress. These are concepts we take for granted today.

God's covenant with Abraham changed history forever. God called Abraham out of this meaningless cycle. He called him to leave his former way of life and start a new one. He gave him a hope and a future promise. He gave him a destiny. Suddenly life had meaning and purpose. History harbored progress, and individual people seemed significant. When the God of the universe revealed his universal strategy of redemption through *one man*—Abraham—each person had potential to affect history. Each individual was significant, accountable, and responsible.

It's hard for us to appreciate how transforming these ideas were four thousand years ago. As Cahill reminds us, these concepts were gifts from the Jews, or perhaps more correctly, they were gifts of God's blessings to the nations, through the Jews. As another example, consider God's laws as revealed in the Commandments (Exod. 20:1–17). God handed the Ten Commandments to Israel, yet today these laws bless and guide nations around the world. They provide a sure, time-tested foundation for moral and just societies.

A Way in the Darkest Hour

Overall, the Old Testament unfolds God's worldwide plan of redemption through his chosen nation. It's a story marked with successes and failures. David's prayer in Psalm 67 and Solomon's temple-dedication prayer in 2 Chronicles 6 demonstrate that Israel initially understood its purpose and destiny. Yet as God's people do still today, time and again Israel disobeyed and neglected God. It often became arrogant and haughty and suffered God's punishment.

Forgetting its purpose to bless, Israel often scorned the nations. By the time of Jesus' arrival, Israel had drifted so far away from its purpose that what Jesus saw in the temple in Jerusalem provoked him to this angry indictment of the religious establishment: "Is it not written: 'My house will be called a house of prayer for *all nations*'? But you have made it 'a den of robbers'" (Mark 11:17, author italics).

Jesus knew that the temple was to be a house of prayer, not just for Israel, but for all nations. Yet Israel had lost its way. It had strayed from God's plan, and as a result, it couldn't bless others. But despite human waywardness, God's plan moved forward. Even in Israel's darkest hours as a nation, God prepared the way for Jesus the Messiah—the light of the world (John 8:12)—to bring redemption to Israel and all nations. What Israel's prophet Isaiah had written about his own nation is true of us all: "We all, like sheep, have gone astray, each of us has turned to his own way; and the LORD has laid on him the iniquity of us all" (Isa. 53:6). Through Jesus, the full scope and meaning of God's redeeming love to the nations would be unleashed in power and humility.

DISCOVERY QUESTIONS
A Nation's Response to the Promise

God said he'd lavishly bless Israel, but he attached the condition of obedience to his commands. By studying the following verses, you'll learn more about the nation's responsibility to follow God's ways. As you study, think about how obedience could have been a joyful response to his blessing rather than just a set of rules to keep.

1. Read Deuteronomy 7:7–8. God is speaking about Israel. Why did God choose these people? What was his choice *not* based on?

    _____

    _____

2. From what did God save (redeem) these people?

    _____

3. Read Genesis 18:17–19, Deuteronomy 4:5–9, 39–40, and 28:9–14. What does God expect his chosen people to do?

    _____

    _____

4. What consequences will follow Israel's obedience?

    _____

    _____

    _____

    _____

5. What will the watching nations learn about Israel when they see its obedience? What will they learn about God?

    _____

    _____

    _____

    _____

6. How might God's blessing upon Israel touch your nation?

    _____

    _____

    _____

KEY POINTS TO REMEMBER

Israel's Role in Review

1. God chose to bless the nation of Israel so that it could bless other nations.
2. If Israel obeyed God's instructions (laws), it would be blessed. If the nation disobeyed, it would reap destruction.
3. When obedient and blessed, Israel served as a model and a messenger, proclaiming to the nations the existence of the one, sovereign God.

CLOSING THOUGHTS
You're a Star!

When the apostle Paul illustrated the relationship between the nation of Israel in the Old Testament and the church in the New Testament, he used an olive tree with many branches (Rom. 11:11–24). God's chosen people Israel is the true olive tree, and the seed of this tree is Abraham. Because of unbelief in God, branches of the natural olive tree were broken off, and branches from another tree—a wild olive tree—were grafted into their place. These grafted-in branches represent the church. Together with believing Jews, we've been grafted into God's chosen tree and belong to the true nation of Israel, with Abraham as our forefather.

When Abraham looked up into the clear night sky and saw countless stars, he remembered God's promise to him, that his offspring would be as numerous as the stars in the heavens (Gen. 15:5). Considering that we are now part of the true tree, one of those "stars" he was looking at was you! We've inherited an amazing legacy. All of the promises that God made to Abraham and his descendants, as well as the responsibilities and obligations, now apply to the church. We're to be a channel of blessing to a broken world.

PERSONAL APPLICATION
Make Me a Blessing

Just as God blessed Israel, he wants to bless you and your nation. Use the following questions to ponder how he could bless others through you.

1. God purposefully used one of the most broken nations on earth to reflect his power and glory to the world. The Bible teaches that God uses the weak things of this world so that "no one may boast" and he may receive the glory (1 Cor. 1:26–29). Reflect on your life. To what were you "enslaved" before God redeemed you? (See Rom. 6:15–23.) How has he healed, restored, and blessed you?

_____

_____

_____

_____

2. God's redemption of Israel from slavery was profound and dramatic.
    It was miraculous so the watching nations would know God did it.
    Has God used his transforming work in your life as a witness to oth-
    ers? If so, how? If you can't pinpoint an incident, how would you like
    for him to use you in the future?

    _____

    _____

    _____

    _____

3. Like Israel, you can be a blessing. You can use your life, gifts, talents,
    and abilities to reflect God's glory to others. Prayerfully think about
    your everyday life. What is a simple but ongoing thing you could do
    to share your talents and/or abilities with others?

    _____

    _____

4. What role will obedience play in blessing others?

    _____

    _____

5. Write a prayer to God, expressing your desire to bless others because
    he has blessed you.

    _____

    _____

    _____

    _____

    _____

A PRACTICAL RESPONSE
Blessing Others

When we think of blessing others—especially the many people in a nation—we can feel overwhelmed by the needs and possibilities. But a little blessing can hold great influence, if given in the Lord's name. Consider how you could share small blessings for big results. Try any or all of the following suggestions.

Start a Blessing Campaign

On a sheet of paper or a whiteboard (for a group discussion), brainstorm at least ten ways you could bless your community, especially those who live apart from God. These could be "small" actions like taking food to a shut-in, collecting pennies for the poor, working one day at a camp for disabled children, volunteering to make and distribute flyers for a struggling business, donating part of your savings to a soup kitchen, etc.

Choose one idea and pledge to do it in the next few weeks. If you're in a group study, report back about the results. How did the recipient(s) respond? How did you feel? Were you able to share anything about your faith in God? If so, what happened?

Also consider starting a "blessing campaign" at your church or organization. Encourage everyone to bestow a small blessing on a non-Christian person or group, during a designated time period. Then host a "testimony time" to talk about the results and thank God for his blessings.

Pray for Peace

Israel often appears in news reports these days, especially because of its needs, conflicts, and accomplishments. Gather up news articles about Israel—both its struggles and triumphs—from the Internet, newspapers, magazines, and other sources. This week, devote time to praying for the peace of Jerusalem (Ps. 122:6). Pray also that God would raise up Christians to share the gospel with Jewish people, and that many hearts would be open to the Messiah.

Consult the Map

In addition to praying for Israel, consult the map of your nation that you created in session 1. Intercede for its brokenness and ask God to increase its blessings. Keep notes and clippings on progress or downfalls in the areas of brokenness that you've listed, and pray about these developments, too.

The next session: *how Jesus forms the center of God's redemptive plan*

Jesus, the Center of God's Plan

The planets...all need a central sun to hold them together, to keep them wheeling in good order, to bequeath them shape and meaning," observes the writer and clergyman Walter Wangerin, Jr.

He also says that history needs a center. "But if that center is empty ...it cannot hold. Things fly apart into absurdity." According to the Bible, history's center is Jesus—his life and death on the cross. "The creator put a cross in the very center of human history—to be its center, forever," explains Wangerin. "It is the person and passion of Jesus Christ which defines us; and because of him we [and history] no longer go down to nothing. Our end is the beginning of a perfect union with God."[4]

Isn't that good news? With Jesus as the center of history, we find meaning for our lives and hope for our nations. We look forward to eternal life in heaven after our bodies die and significant healing for our lives and nations now.

In this session you'll learn about Jesus as the centerpiece of God's redemptive plan for the world. His sacrificial death on the cross created a way for fallen humanity to regain intimacy with God. This, in turn, opened the door for substantial healing throughout the rest of creation. It unleashed the floodgates of blessing, pouring out healing to individuals and to the nations.

KEY WORDS TO KNOW
Ancient Words, Powerful Words

Sin

A person sins when he or she voluntarily departs from God's intentions or disobeys his commands. Used as a noun, the word *sin* describes any action, attitude, or thought that runs counter to God's revealed commands or intentions. To sin is to violate God's law. Because of the Fall, the Bible declares that "all have sinned" (Rom. 3:23). In fact, the Bible declares that in our flesh we're enslaved to sin (Rom. 6:16–18). Without the redeeming work of Christ on the cross, this violation separates us from a relationship with a holy God and leads to destruction and eternal death.

Atone (Atonement)

To atone is to make amends to someone we've hurt, angered, or offended. An atonement is a payment made to someone as recompense for the wrong done. Our disobedience to God's commands (our sin) has offended and angered him. In the Old Testament, God established a system of animal sacrifices to atone for this disobedience. In the New Testament, God sent his own Son, Jesus, to die on the cross as a final, perfect atoning sacrifice for our sin.

Reconcile (Reconciliation)

To reconcile with someone restores friendship or favor between parties after a conflict. The atoning death of Jesus on the cross forged a reconciliation between God and his fallen creation—a relationship that had been broken as a result of human disobedience and sin.

KEY VERSES TO READ
The Reconciler of All Things

For God was pleased to have all his fullness dwell in [Jesus], and through him to reconcile to himself all things, whether things on earth or things in heaven, by making peace through his blood, shed on the cross.

—*Colossians 1:19–20*

1. How does this passage describe Jesus? What does this description reveal about him?

   _____

   _____

2. Why did Jesus die on the cross?

   _____

   _____

3. What does the term "all things" refer to in these verses?

   _____

   _____

4. How was the reconciliation between God and "all things" made possible?

   _____

   _____

BIBLICAL INSIGHTS
Who in the World Is Jesus?

Somebody once commented that Jesus Christ was either the Son of God or the biggest hoax in history. Today, as in the past, Jesus and his claim to divinity evoke strong reactions. He sounds scandalous. "The scandal of the cross [and Jesus] is that [they are] so foolish," comments author Dan Allender. "God, the infinite Creator, becomes a perfect sacrifice for the sake of a twisted human soul. He not only dies, but does so as a public spectacle of shame."[5]

Centuries before, God's promise to Israel also seemed foolish. The Lord pledged to bless Israel—and to bless all nations on earth through Israel. However, this promise hinged upon Israel's obedience to God's commands. As Israel lived according to them, it would be a blessed and prosperous model nation.

However, as a result of humanity's fallen sinful nature, Israel found obedience impossible. The people repeatedly turned away from God and worshiped idols. As a result they faced God's wrath and discipline. Yet in one of their darkest hours as a nation, when Israel had fallen so far that no hope for recovery looked possible, the prophet Jeremiah offered comforting words from the Lord:

> "The time is coming," declares the LORD,
>   "when I will make a new covenant
>   with the house of Israel....
> This is the covenant I will make with the house of Israel....
> I will put my law in their minds
>   and write it on their hearts.
> I will be their God,
>   and they will be my people.
> No longer will a man teach his neighbor,
>   or a man his brother, saying, 'Know the LORD,'
> because they will all know me,
>   from the least of them to the greatest....
> For I will forgive their wickedness
>   and will remember their sins no more."
>
> —*Jeremiah 31:31–34*

God knew that because of humanity's sinful nature, Israel couldn't fully uphold the covenant agreement. Yet he is a holy, perfect Creator, whose nature hates sin (Jer. 44:4) and punishes it (Rom. 1:18; 2:5–9).

Without atonement, no fellowship with him is possible. Consequently God established the Old Testament system of sacrifices that shed the blood of unflawed animals "to make atonement" for the people's sins (Lev. 17:11).

At the same time, these sacrifices pointed ahead to when God would forgive humanity's wickedness once and for all. He would reveal a new chapter in his grand redemptive plan. It would allow people to be in right relationship with their Creator. He accomplished this through Jesus.

Jesus Paid the Price

Jesus, the Son of God, the second person of the Trinity and the creator of everything (John 1:1–14; Col. 1:15, 16), stands at the center of God's plan for the nations (Mark 1:10–12; John 1:1–3; 3:16). Jesus fulfilled God's promise prophesied by the prophet Jeremiah. He accomplished something that animal sacrifices never could. He paid the penalty for sin and disobedience with a resounding finality.

Through the Cross, God revealed both the terrible depth of his hatred toward sin and his unfathomable love and compassion for his broken creation. He sacrificed his beloved Son's life on behalf of the world. Some false religions demand the sacrifice of children for the gods. But on the cross God sacrificed his Son for us!

The Old Testament foreshadowed this event. Recall Abraham preparing to sacrifice his son Isaac in Genesis 22. He bound his hands, laid him on the altar, and raised his knife. At the last possible moment, God spared Isaac's life by providing a substitute sacrifice, a ram, to take the place of his son. Two thousand years later God provided another substitute offering, the Lamb of God, who would die in place of not just one person at one time but for all people and all time.

Through his sacrificial death on the cross, Jesus paid the penalty for our sin and provided a righteousness we couldn't secure for ourselves. God poured his wrath against human sinfulness on Jesus. He died the death we deserved. God also credited to his people the righteousness of Jesus. When God looks at us, he sees Christ's perfect obedience. Therefore "those who trust in Jesus stand before God, not simply cleansed of sin, but clothed in the spotless righteousness of Christ."[6]

Accepting and Living the Gift

What is left for us to do? Simply to accept this amazing gift of grace by repenting of our sin, acknowledging Jesus as Savior, and receiving his atoning sacrifice and righteousness. The apostle Paul summarized this process in a passage that's central to the gospel:

> But now a righteousness from God, apart from law, has been made known, to which the Law and the Prophets testify. This righteousness from God comes through faith in Jesus Christ to all who believe. There is no difference, for all have sinned and fall short of the glory of God, and are justified freely by his grace through the redemption that came by Christ Jesus.
>
> —Romans 3:21–24

Through this atoning sacrifice, Jesus made peace and fellowship with God possible again. Once this primary relationship with God was restored, then substantial healing could occur in secondary relationships—our relationships to other people and to creation. As the apostle Paul stated in this session's key verses, "God was pleased…to reconcile to himself *all things*, whether things on earth or things in heaven, by making peace though [Christ's] blood, shed on the cross (Col. 1:19–20, author's italics).

Through Christ, humanity entered into a new era of history. Christ's shed blood holds the key to the restoration of all things. Today the blessing of God through Jesus has been extended to every nation on earth, bringing hope for healing and restoration. The good news of Jesus has been preached to the people of many nations, and everywhere this has occurred, many have responded. Before God brings down the curtain on history, "a great multitude that no one could count, from every nation, tribe, people and language" (Rev. 7:9) will be drawn to Christ. Thus Abraham's offspring will bless all the nations.

DISCOVERY QUESTIONS
What's in It for You?

Jesus died for all humanity, and that means he died for you. God sacrificed his Son to atone for your sins and redeem you. In this section use the study questions to explore God's redemptive act even more.

1. Begin by reading Romans 8:6–8. What is a sinful person unable to do?

     _____

     _____

2. According to Romans 3:23, who is considered a sinner?

     _____

     _____

3. Based on Romans 2:5–11 and Ephesians 2:1–3, what is the consequence of sin, which is rebellion against God?

     _____

     _____

4. Read Ephesians 2:4–5. While we were still sinners and hostile toward God, what did he do for us?

     _____

     _____

5. According to these verses, what did Jesus Christ's death accomplish?

     Romans 8:1–4

     _____

     _____

     2 Corinthians 5:21

     _____

     _____

Ephesians 1:7

_____

_____

Revelation 1:5–6

_____

_____

6. What are the benefits for those who accept Christ's sacrificial death
    on the cross as an atonement for their sins?

    2 Corinthians 5:17–19

    _____

    _____

    Ephesians 2:4–7

    _____

    _____

7. Turn to Jeremiah 31:31–34, Luke 22:19–20, and Hebrews 10:1–18.
    Read them carefully. Then in your own words, state the differences
    between the "old covenant" in Exodus 6:6–7 and 19:3–6 and the "new
    covenant" referred to in these passages. Why was the new covenant
    necessary?

    _____

    _____

    _____

    _____

    _____

8. Take time to prayerfully meditate on the following passages, which
    discuss additional benefits of our salvation through Jesus. Which of
    these benefits are most meaningful to you? Circle them.

John 3:16

Romans 8:1–4

2 Corinthians 5:17

Galatians 3:26–29; 4:6–7

Ephesians 2:11–13, 19

KEY POINTS TO REMEMBER
The Man Who Made a Difference

1. The ultimate barrier to God's redemptive plan for the nations is human sin.
2. Through the Cross, Jesus paid the penalty for sin and provided a righteousness we couldn't secure for ourselves.
3. When we accept this amazing gift of atonement, our sins are forgiven and "remembered no more" (see Jer. 31:34) and Christ credits his righteousness to us.
4. When God restores our primary relationship with him, a door opens for substantial healing and restoration of the whole person. He also offers healing for our secondary relationships with others and creation.
5. The healing through Christ's shed blood is comprehensive, covering everything broken by the Fall.

CLOSING THOUGHTS
Christ's Enduring Kingdom

Hundreds of years before the birth of Jesus, the mightiest king on earth had a remarkable, recurring dream. His name was Nebuchadnezzar—ruler of the vast Babylonian Empire. The king was greatly disturbed by his dream and demanded that his royal magicians and enchanters interpret it. When they proved unable, the king called for a young Jewish exile named Daniel, a God-fearing, wise man with an unshakable faith in the Lord. With God's help, Daniel was able to interpret the dream, which proved to be a prophesy of a coming King whose power would surpass even that of the great Nebuchadnezzar. Here is how Daniel 2:31–44 records the exciting moment when Daniel reveals and then interprets the dream:

> You looked, O king, and there before you stood a large statue—an enormous, dazzling statue, awesome in appearance. The head of the statue was made of pure gold, its chest and arms of silver, its belly and thighs of bronze, its legs of iron, its feet partly of iron and partly of baked clay. While you were watching, a rock was cut out, but not by human hands. It struck the statue on its feet of iron and clay and smashed them. Then the iron, the clay, the bronze, the silver and the gold were broken to pieces at the same time and became like chaff on a threshing floor in the summer. The wind swept them away without leaving a trace. But the rock that struck the statue became a huge mountain and filled the whole earth.
>
> This was the dream, and now we will interpret it to the king. You, O king, are the king of kings. The God of heaven has given you dominion and power and might and glory…. You are that head of gold.
>
> After you, another kingdom will rise, inferior to yours [the Medo-Persian Empire]. Next, a third kingdom, one of bronze, will rule over the whole earth [the Grecian

Empire]. Finally, there will be a fourth kingdom, strong as iron—for iron breaks and smashes everything—and as iron breaks things to pieces, so it will crush and break all the others [the Roman Empire]....

In the time of [the Roman] kings, the God of heaven will set up a kingdom that will never be destroyed, nor will it be left to another people. It will crush all those kingdoms and bring them to an end, but it will itself endure forever.

As followers of Jesus Christ, we ourselves are subjects of that kingdom that will endure forever. Jesus himself is the small rock not cut by human hands. Since his death and resurrection more than two thousand years ago, his influence and power have spread across the globe. Today, millions of people from countless nations claim to be his followers and continue to spread word of his fame. His kingdom truly has grown into a mighty mountain filling the whole earth. As the prophet Isaiah said, "Of the increase of his government and peace there will be no end" (Isa. 9:7). His kingdom will increase until all the kingdoms of man are subdued and pay allegiance to the true King of kings. Truly Jesus stands unchallenged as the most significant life in human history and the center of God's redemptive plan for mankind.

PERSONAL APPLICATION
In Your Own Words and Life

Before finishing this session, ponder how God's gift of forgiveness touches your life and the nations. The following questions can guide your thoughts and conclusions.

1. In your own words, describe why Jesus is the center of God's redemptive plan for the nations and creation.

_____

_____

2. If Jesus is the center of God's redemption, then he's central to those
    who accept him as Savior. What might be the characteristics of
    someone who makes Jesus the center of his or her life? List three to
    five attributes.

    _____

    _____

    _____

3. From the list in question 2, circle a characteristic that already exists
    in your life. Underline a characteristic that you most need to develop.
    How can you cultivate the attribute that you underlined?

    _____

    _____

    _____

    _____

4. How can you make Christ the center of your life on a daily basis?
    Write down some practical and realistic ideas.

    _____

    _____

    _____

    _____

5. Write a prayer to Christ, stating what you appreciate about his sacri-
    fice on the cross and how it affects you.

    _____

    _____

    _____

    _____

    _____

    _____

A PRACTICAL RESPONSE

Christ at the Center

How has Christ's atonement affected your nation? How can it make a difference in the future? Answer these questions by completing one or more of the following activities.

Make a Spiritual Timeline

From your or your group's knowledge, create a spiritual timeline of your nation for the last century (or a longer time period if you prefer). On the timeline, answer these questions:

1. What values touched your nation through the decades?
2. What religious groups have predominated?
3. Where has biblical Christianity affected the nation, if at all?

Don't worry about making your timeline exact. It can be roughed out by hand and represent your "best guess."

Where Is Christ Today?

Looking at the timeline, consider these questions:

1. How would you describe your nation's history with Christ?
2. What is your nation's relationship with Christ today?
3. Does your nation place Christ at its center? Why, or why not?

Write your answers on the timeline. You can post the timeline next to the map created in session 1. This will provide a more comprehensive look at your nation's spiritual and other needs and serve as a reminder as you work through the next sessions.

Pray On

Continue praying for your nation by referring to the map from session 1 and the timeline you just created. Focus on your nation's need to place Christ at the center of its life and future.

The next session: *the present role of the church in God's plan of redemption*

God's Purpose for the Church

Insook Prison Hospital, a notorious jail, lies on the outskirts of a crowded Southeast Asian city. The hospital admits prisoners suffering from various illnesses, but they receive the barest necessities and virtually no treatment. Sicknesses typically grow worse.

In early 1999, Dr. Chitko Aung, a general practitioner, and Martha Nyut, a dental nurse (their names have been changed), sensed the Lord calling them to this forsaken place. They mobilized a team of volunteers from a local church who were willing to clean the hospital and minister to the prisoners. Together the doctor and nurse visited the prison authorities and explained their plan. The authorities acted perplexed by the unusual request, but they reluctantly granted permission, warning the volunteers not to speak about their Christian faith.

Later, when the church members arrived at the hospital, the horrible sights and smells overwhelmed them. The wards were filthy, and the toilets appeared never to have been cleaned. The workers could only stay for an hour because of the sickening odor. Despite this the group returned repeatedly with cleaning materials and scrubbed the place. The doctor and nurse also tended to medical needs, but they never spoke to the prisoners about their faith.

The prison authorities and staff were so touched, they invited the church members to return anytime to clean the wards and treat the prisoners. They also gave the volunteers permission to speak freely about Jesus. Through unconditional love these Christians brought hope and healing to a forgotten and neglected corner of their society.

When the church first appeared two thousand years ago, it proved a revolutionary force in society because the members carried a stunning concept into everyday life. Christians spoke of a God who loved his people and sacrificed for them. In turn, his followers demonstrated their love to one another and to others through personal sacrifice. Such mercy and compassion, especially toward strangers, was unprecedented. Through the centuries, wherever the church has lived this vision, entire nations have been impacted by Christ's love.

In this session, you'll learn how God raised up the church to be his principal agent for advancing redemption, blessing, and healing to the nations.

KEY WORD TO KNOW
Which Church Is It?

Church

The Greek word for church in the New Testament is *ecclesia*, meaning "assembly." The same word is used for both the church universal and a local congregation.

In the universal sense, the church is the living, worldwide group of redeemed people who've placed their faith in Christ for the forgiveness of sins and have been adopted as God's children (Eph. 1:22–23; 4:4–6).

In the local sense, New Testament writers often refer to specific local congregations, such as the church at Jerusalem in Acts 8:1. Local churches are community-based expressions of the worldwide church. These churches meet regularly for worship, fellowship, and service. In the locations where they gather, local churches serve as small-scale representations of the universal church.

KEY VERSES TO READ

A Chosen People, a Holy Nation

But you are a chosen people, a royal priesthood, a holy nation, a people belonging to God, that you may declare the praises of him who called you out of darkness into his wonderful light. Once you were not a people, but now you are the people of God; once you had not received mercy, but now you have received mercy.

—*1 Peter 2:9–10*

1. In Exodus 19:5–6, God spoke to Moses about Israel. What are the similarities between this Old Testament passage and the New Testament claims in 1 Peter 2:9–10? List them.

   _____

   _____

   _____

2. A follower of Christ and a Jew, Peter wrote to the Gentiles, describing them as "the people of God." Why was this description significant? See God's promise to the Israelites in Exodus 6:7 for insight.

   _____

   _____

   _____

3. In the passage above, Peter indicated that God blessed these Gentile Christians for a purpose. What was that purpose?

   _____

   _____

4. How did this purpose relate to God's redemptive plan for the nations?

   _____

   _____

   _____

BIBLICAL INSIGHTS

Building a New Kind of Nation

After Jesus died on the cross and rose again, he established his church to carry God's redemption to all nations. He raised up the church as a new and holy nation—a nation unlike any other in the world. Its members were not identified by a common ethnicity or geographic location. Instead the church was comprised of people from many nations who put their trust in Jesus Christ.

The New Testament describes the church as an extension of Israel, God's chosen people of the Old Testament. The Lord enlarged Israel's borders beyond Abraham's blood descendants. Through faith in Christ, Gentile believers joined the covenant's promise. The apostle Paul explained this supernatural process, using the metaphor of a building:

> For [Jesus] himself is our peace, who has made the two one and has destroyed the barrier, the dividing wall of hostility.... His purpose was to create in himself one new man out of the two, thus making peace....
>
> Consequently, you are no longer foreigners and aliens, but fellow citizens with God's people and members of God's household, built on the foundation of the apostles and prophets, with Christ Jesus himself as the chief cornerstone. In him the whole building is joined together and rises to become a holy temple in the Lord. And in him you too are being built together to become a dwelling in which God lives by his Spirit.
>
> —*Ephesians 2:14–22*

Today God's promise to bless all nations carries on through the church. At the end of Jesus' time on earth, he instructed a small band of followers, who became founders of the church, about their responsibility. These instructions appear in the Great Commission, recorded in Matthew 28:18–20. With this Commission, Jesus commanded his followers—then and now—to "make disciples of all nations" (vs. 19).

It's important to note the similarities between Jesus' Great Commission to his followers and God's promise to Abraham in Genesis 12:1–3. Both sets of instructions focus on the nations. As with Israel, God chose the church to serve the nations, and he's worked through this body of believers for two thousand years.

As with Israel, the historical contribution of the church has been flawed. It's even responsible for several atrocities. The Crusades of the eleventh, twelfth, and thirteenth centuries, which destroyed and embittered many Muslims, were wrongly conducted in the name of Christ. The Inquisition was created by the church to root out heretics, originally by means of "inquests." By the fifteenth century it had evolved into its most infamous, violent form, eventually operating in most of Europe and in Latin America. European antisemitism over the centuries was "justified" by wrongful church interpretation of the New Testament. In addition, numerous religious conflicts often had political as well as religious aspects, like the bitter conflict between Protestants and Catholics in Ireland.

Yet, even with the church's brokenness and failure, God still works through it to bring healing, hope, and redemption to the nations. Despite the church's failures, many Christians have earnestly followed Christ's teachings. Consequently the ages also ring with the "good works" that Jesus modeled and the apostle Paul encouraged in believers (Eph. 2:10). The apostle James also admonished Christians that faith without works is dead (James 2:14–26), and though good works aren't the way to salvation, they're the natural result of love for and obedience to God.

When Christians have followed biblical teachings, the church's life and outreach have profoundly affected the world. For example:

The church is God's primary instrument to carry the gospel. It has preached the message of Christ's finished work for our salvation. Throughout the generations, people have discovered new life in Christ through the witness of local churches and missionary outreaches.

The church is an agency of God's compassion. In the human race's fallen condition, cruelty is common. Throughout history people have practiced this cruelty both by neglect and design. Into this depraved world, the church has carried Christ's command to "love your neighbor as yourself" (Mark 12:31). It has manifested God's compassion by creating hospitals, charity houses, food kitchens, orphanages, literacy programs, technical schools, and other ministries to help the poor and disenfranchised.

The church promotes the sacredness of human life. The church believes that God creates all human life in his image; therefore it believes in the sacredness of human life and the eternal significance of individuals from all walks of life. The church, more often than not, has stood up for the poor and downcast. It has condemned infanticide and abortion. Despite the unbiblical subjugation of peoples and women by some Christians throughout history, the church has promoted the dignity of women and has been instrumental in working against slavery and racial prejudice, in keeping with Christ's true teaching.

The church distributes God's Word around the world. It has translated the Bible into thousands of languages. The church has also worked for universal education so both peasants and clerics could read the Word of God themselves. Because of the church, schools have been established around the world.

The church believes in the sacredness of work. It recognizes the dignity of labor. The work ethic that flowed out of the Protestant Reformation ignited a transformation that produced the free-market system and raised nations out of poverty.

The church helped initiate modern science and technology. This was born from the church's biblical worldview. Many founders of modern science were devout men of faith. These early scientists understood that God reveals himself in creation and through Scripture. So they examined creation to learn more about the Creator. They believed that creation is observably rational and orderly because God himself is orderly (Isa. 45:18–19) and that people, made in a creative God's image, could apply creativity and innovation to the orderly cosmos.

This freedom of inquiry unlocked doors to many discoveries and innovations. New medicines were developed to save lives. New forms of agriculture increased the food supply and helped fight the effects of natural disasters, such as droughts or floods.

The church contributed to political reform. Regained biblical concepts of the fallen, sinful nature of man and the priesthood of all believers and renewed understanding of God's laws led Christians to create new political structures during the Reformation—structures that diffused power, both in churches and civil society. Christians believed all legitimate laws ultimately came from God, and that earthly kings and rulers were under the authority of—and accountable to—God's eternal and transcendent law. They taught that the "law is king." In other words, both kings and commoners were subject to the laws of their nations. The legal application of biblical principles contributed to a great movement for freedom and justice.

These and other actions illustrate God's gifts to the nations through the church. Yet this is not a completed history. At the end of the age, all nations will be blessed through the church. The best is yet to come.

DISCOVERY QUESTIONS
A Kingdom of Priests

Open your Bible to read more about the church. Then answer the following questions about its role in the world.

1. Read Galatians 3:26–29 and Ephesians 2:11–20; 3:6. In these passages, the apostle Paul explains how the Gentiles became "Abraham's seed" and "heirs together with Israel…in the promise in Christ Jesus." How did they earn these descriptions?

_____

_____

_____

2. A priest is someone who serves as an intermediary between God and humanity. Keeping this in mind, turn to Exodus 19:6 and Revelation 5:9–10. Who is described as a "kingdom of priests" in these passages? Why would they be given this title?

_____

_____

_____

3. How could the church's priestly role contribute to God's redemptive plan for the nations? See the key verses for this session, 1 Peter 2:9–10.

_____

_____

_____

_____

_____

4. Read the following verses. How is the church described in each? Which is most meaningful to you, and why?

John 10:14–16

_____

_____

Galatians 6:14–16

_____

_____

Ephesians 1:22–23

_____

_____

Ephesians 2:19–22

_____

_____

Ephesians 3:14–19

_____

_____

1 Peter 2:9

_____

_____

Revelation 19:7–8

_____

_____

5. Read 1 Corinthians 12:4–28 and Ephesians 4:10–13. What is the source of unity within the church? Where can we observe diversity in the church?

_____

_____

_____

6. From what you've studied in this section, how is the church meant to function?

_____

_____

_____

KEY POINTS TO REMEMBER
The Church in Review

1. God established a new covenant through Christ's shed blood on the cross. Through this covenant, the new "chosen nation" is the church.
2. The church advances God's plan of redemption, bringing hope and blessing to the nations.
3. In addition to sharing the gospel with the nations, the church has been used in many capacities to influence and better the world.

CLOSING THOUGHTS
A Powerful Agent of Change

Despite flaws and failings, local churches are more strategic to the transformation of a society than its leaders, president, legislators, businessmen, educators, or scientists! That's because God has uniquely blessed the local church to carry his plan of redemption and healing to the nations.

For this transformation to occur, the mere physical presence of churches is not enough. Each local church must understand its role and boldly take God's truth into all spheres of society. A church can train its members to be godly citizens and leaders. These people, in turn, can influence families, communities, and nations for the kingdom of God.

Unless local churches disciple their people to be "salt and light" (Matt. 5:13–16) within these spheres, the nations will not be discipled. How will you join this great and powerful commission?

PERSONAL APPLICATION
You and Your Local Church

It helps to recognize our feelings about the church and its local congregations before we can work within it. With these questions, reflect on your relationship to your local church(es).

1. What do you appreciate about the universal church in general?

    _____

    _____

    _____

2. How do you feel about the church's flawed history? Its good works? Why?

    _____

    _____

    _____

    _____

3. What do you appreciate about the local church? What frustrates you? Why?

    _____

    _____

    _____

    _____

4. Do you belong to a local church group? If so, how would you describe it?

_____

_____

_____

_____

5. What are your local church's strengths and weaknesses?

_____

_____

_____

_____

6. How would you describe your church's attitude toward community involvement? Toward reaching the world's nations?

_____

_____

_____

_____

7. Is there anything about the local church that might hinder you from participating in its outreach to your community? If so, how can you overcome these hindrances?

_____

_____

_____

_____

8. What positive aspects about the local church will encourage you to reach out to your community and the world?

_____

_____

_____

_____

A PRACTICAL RESPONSE

Blessing Your Community

This study stresses that the church is God's principally ordained agent for advancing his plan of redemption, bringing hope and blessing to the nations. Now make this statement personal: *The local church you attend is God's principally ordained agent for advancing his plan of redemption, bringing hope and blessing to your community.*

Continue with this idea by answering the following questions.

1. Does the leadership of your congregation understand the local church's role in your community? If so, how do you know this? If not, how can you help them understand this?

_____

_____

_____

_____

2. Think about your community. What are its most significant areas of brokenness? How do these areas compare to your nation's brokenness? (See the list you made in session 1.)

_____

_____

_____

_____

_____

3. Consider your involvement in the local church. List three or four things you or your family could do through the church to minister to your community's brokenness.

_____

_____

_____

_____

4. Select one thing from question 3 that you'd like to do. Write it down below. This week, ask God how to begin implementing this outreach.

_____

_____

_____

_____

The next session: *the glory of the nations*

The Glory of the Nations

The pastor of a small church in Beira, Mozambique, stood somberly at his rough-hewn pulpit. He looked out over the congregants, their tired, dark faces lit dimly by a single candle burning near the altar. The church members met in the dingy basement of an old, run-down colonial building. There was no electricity, just a cold dirt floor under their feet. No glass covered the window openings. Nothing muffled the sounds of a bustling street during their Wednesday-night prayer meeting.

As the pastor closed the service, he recalled the Bible passage they'd read that evening. It was Revelation 21:22–27, which foretold the glory and honor of the nations brought into the new Jerusalem at the end of the age. *What,* he wondered, *is the glory and honor of this nation?*

In his opinion, Mozambique was a poor nation, and it would probably always be impoverished. His country brimmed with sorrow and broken dreams. Not long ago the nation had been released from Portuguese colonization, but shortly afterward a terrible civil war erupted. Other nations were blessed—nations the pastor had only heard about—but this nation wasn't. It wasn't even close.

Then suddenly the pastor remembered how God promised that a broken, poor slave nation—the nation of Israel—would bless the world. *Was this God speaking to him, encouraging him with things yet to come?* His spirit lightened. *Maybe God had a plan for Mozambique after all, a plan that would someday bless this struggling nation...and maybe this little church could be part of that plan.* The possibility sparked hope in his heart. He smiled as he bowed his head to pray.

In this session you'll glimpse the blessings God holds in store for the nations when he returns to the earth and the role we play in that plan.

KEY WORDS TO KNOW
The New and Improved Future

Revelation

A revelation, or a "revealing," uncovers or brings to light something previously hidden. Throughout history God supernaturally revealed to humans many things about himself, his purposes, and his plans. Under the guidance of his Spirit, men recorded this information in the various books of the Bible.

The Revelation to John, also known simply as Revelation, or sometimes, the Apocalypse, is the only book in the New Testament that focuses entirely on future events. These prophecies will be fulfilled at the end of the age when Christ returns, an event known as the Second Coming. The apostle John wrote Revelation.

New Jerusalem

The "new Jerusalem" or "heavenly Jerusalem" is referred to three times in the New Testament (Heb. 12:22; Rev. 3:12; 21:2). (In the Hebrews passage it is also called "Mount Zion.") It refers to God's heavenly dwelling, or the throne of Christ the King. Revelation describes the heavenly Jerusalem as the place of God's presence.

The new Jerusalem also calls to mind the city of Jerusalem on earth, in Israel. This city has enjoyed historical and spiritual significance since the days of Abraham, when it was called Salem, "the city of peace." God formed his famous covenant with Abraham near this site. Later Jerusalem became the capital of the Jewish nation and the home of the temple, a holy place of worship. This earthbound temple served as a "type" or model of the true, permanent temple of God in heaven.

KEY VERSES TO READ

A Glimpse into Glory

> After this I looked and there before me was a great multitude that no one could count, from every nation, tribe, people and language, standing before the throne and in front of the Lamb. They were wearing white robes and were holding palm branches in their hands. And they cried out in a loud voice:
>
> "Salvation belongs to our God,
>   who sits on the throne,
>   and to the Lamb."
>
> —Revelation 7:9–10

> Therefore,
> "they are before the throne of God
>   and serve him day and night in his temple;
> and he who sits on the throne will spread his tent over them.
> Never again will they hunger;
>   never again will they thirst.
> The sun will not beat upon them,
>   nor any scorching heat.
> For the Lamb at the center of the throne will be their shepherd;
>   he will lead them to springs of living water.
> And God will wipe away every tear from their eyes."
>
> —Revelation 7:15–17

1. These verses from Revelation peek into the future. After the return of Jesus, who will be "standing before the throne and in front of the Lamb" (vs. 9)?

   _____

   _____

2. The people in Revelation 7:9–10 wear white robes. Read Isaiah 1:18 and Revelation 19:6–8. Then, in your own words, describe the meaning of these robes.

   _____

   _____

3. What are the different words used to describe Jesus in the verses above, and in Revelation 22:12–24? Why would each description be important?

   _____

   _____

   _____

4. Based on the verses you've read for this section, what specific blessings will the nations enjoy after Jesus returns?

   _____

   _____

   _____

BIBLICAL INSIGHTS
A Marriage Worth Waiting For

When an engaged man and woman truly love each other, there's no one quite so eager to get married. When Christ returns, the Bible teaches that, among other things, he's coming back to be wed! The book of Revelation describes this wedding. Jesus is the groom, and the church is his dearly beloved bride (the bride of Christ). The church is God's treasured possession, and we can joyously anticipate the bridegroom's certain arrival.

> "Hallelujah!
> For our Lord God Almighty reigns.
> Let us rejoice and be glad
> and give him glory!
> For the wedding of the Lamb has come,
> and his bride has made herself ready.
> Fine linen, bright and clean,
> was given her to wear."
> (Fine linen stands for the righteous acts of the saints.)
>
> —*Revelation 19:6–8*

In many cultures it's common for a groom to pay a dowry to the bride's father to secure her hand in marriage. The dowry is usually an expensive gift or sum of money. Jesus also paid a dowry to secure our betrothal to him. The apostle Peter described the price he paid: "For you know that it was not with perishable things such as silver or gold that you were redeemed from the empty way of life handed down to you from your forefathers, but with the precious blood of Christ, a lamb without blemish or defect" (1 Pet. 1:18–19). Christ loved us so much, he sacrificed his life to secure our hand in marriage.

It's also common for a bride to spend much time preparing herself for a wedding. In the same way, the church can prepare for her wedding day. Her bridal gown, spun of "fine linen, bright and clean," is "the righteous acts of the saints" (Rev. 19:8). Every righteous act that God's people perform—whether sharing their faith, feeding the hungry, providing shelter for the homeless, clothing the naked, caring for the sick, or visiting those in prison (Matt. 25: 31–46)—adds another brilliant white thread to this wedding dress.

The Light of Reflected Glory

Later in the book of Revelation, the author claims that earthly kings will bring the splendor, glory, and honor of their nations into the heavenly Jerusalem. They will marvel in the light of the Lord's countenance.

> I did not see a temple in the city [the New Jerusalem] because the Lord God Almighty and the Lamb are its temple. The city does not need the sun or the moon to shine on it, for the glory of God gives it light, and the Lamb is its lamp. The nations will walk by its light, and the kings of the earth will bring their splendor into it. On no day will its gates ever be shut for there will be no night there. The glory and honor of the nations will be brought into it.
>
> —*Revelation 21:22–26*

Christ commanded the church to make disciples of all nations so that the glory and honor of each nation could be presented to the Father. The ultimate purpose of history and the destiny of the nations is to glorify and honor God. The Fall distorted the nations, yet beneath the sin, injustice, corruption, and idolatry, a unique core of glory and splendor will shine in God's glory. The glory of each nation will be reflected glory. As the moon reflects the light of the sun, so each nation will uniquely reflect the glory of God.

Each person's divine purpose is fulfilled when he or she lives in relationship with God and obeys his commands. It's the same for each nation. The divine purpose of each nation is revealed as it conforms to God's will, whether in the sphere of law, the arts, education, or government. When the people follow his ways, in heaven they'll bask in his presence.

DISCOVERY QUESTIONS
In the Lord's Presence

Open your Bible to read more about the nations who'll stand in God's presence. Heaven and its inhabitants will be quite a sight! Can you imagine it? Read Psalm 47:1–2, Psalm 67:3–4, Psalm 117, and Revelation 15:2–4, then answer the following questions.

1. At the end of the age, who will be gathered in the presence of Jesus, the King?

_____

_____

2. According to Revelation 15:2–4, what will they be doing?

_____

_____

3. What is the end result of God's history-encompassing plan of redemption?

_____

_____

4. Read Isaiah 60:1–7 and Revelation 21:22–27. What will the kings of the earth bring into the presence of Christ the King?

_____

_____

KEY POINTS TO REMEMBER
At the End of the Age

1. The ultimate purpose of history and the destiny of the nations is to bring glory and honor to God.
2. At the end of time, a great multitude from every nation, tribe, people, and language will stand before the throne of Jesus in the new Jerusalem.
3. At that time, Christ will reign over the nations. The redeemed will see his glory, and they'll worship and praise him.
4. Every righteous act that we perform adds a brilliant white thread to the wedding dress we'll wear as Christ's bride.
5. God wants to bless every nation, so at the end of the age, the unique glory and honor of the nations will be revealed.
6. A nation reveals its glory and honor as it conforms to God's truth in every sphere of life.

CLOSING THOUGHTS
Our Present Task

In his Great Commission (Matt. 28:18–20) Christ commanded his church to "make disciples of all nations...teaching them to obey all I have commanded." Unfortunately, many Christians today have a narrow, fragmented view of this task. Rather than seeking a comprehensive healing of the nations through active, loving engagement in society, much of the church remains on the sidelines, disengaged from its surrounding culture. As a result, many churches have grown weak and anemic, unable to effectively impact or shape their nation.

Yet God's promises are true. The nations will be blessed through the church, and the unique glory and honor of each nation will be revealed. The question is, will the church in our generation be faithful to this mandate? Will it extend God's blessings to the nations? May the answer be a resounding yes!

PERSONAL APPLICATION
Eternity in Your Heart

A heart-touching passage from the ancient book of Ecclesiastes says, "He has made everything beautiful in its time. He has also set eternity in the hearts of men; yet they cannot fathom what God has done from beginning to end" (3:11). Though we don't know everything about the end times, or even understand all that's been revealed, we carry eternity in our hearts. We instinctively long for something beyond our earthly lives and bodies.

Use the following questions to reflect on what's in your heart and on how the end times can affect your life and calling.

1. On a scale of 1 (low interest) to 10 (high interest), what has been your interest in the end times? Why?

_____

_____

_____

_____

2. Using the same scale, what has been your interest in the world's
    nations? Why?

    _____

    _____

    _____

    _____

3. Think about the facts presented in this session. Has anything about
    the nations and end times particularly impressed or interested you? If
    so, what?

    _____

    _____

    _____

    _____

4. How could these facts motivate you toward reaching the nations?

    _____

    _____

    _____

    _____

5. What might hinder your motivation?

    _____

    _____

    _____

    _____

6. How could you develop a passion for the nations so they can stand
    before God's throne at the end of time?

    _____

    _____

_____

7. To seriously pursue the redemption of the nations (or just your nation), how might you need to change your attitudes and lifestyle? How do you feel about this?

_____

A PRACTICAL RESPONSE
Lasting Glory

In this session we've learned that the ultimate destiny of the nations is to bring glory and honor to God. God wants to bless every nation and reveal its unique glory and honor. To explore how God might accomplish this through believers in your nation, complete one or more of the following activities.

Your Nation's Hall of Fame

Draw three vertical columns on a sheet of paper or on a whiteboard. At the top of the first column write "Fame." Then ask, "What are the positive things our nation is famous for among the nations of the world?" To develop this list, consider these questions: What good reputation does your nation have among other nations? What are the positive qualities of the people in your nation? What natural resources, products, services, or artistic endeavors does your nation produce?

Next, write the title "Faith" at the top of the middle column. Across from each characteristic in the first column, suggest how God could use this quality to bring people to saving faith in him. For example, if your nation creates great theater, what could be done? What about the food it produces?

At the top of the third column, write the word "Future." For each famous quality, describe the future if it's (a) used for Christ's glory or (b) unaffected by God's values.

You might want to tack this three-column list near the map and other lists you created in previous lessons, providing a more comprehensive view of your nation's personality.

On Knees for a Nation

In your group or on your own, pray for your nation's qualities listed in the Hall of Fame. Ask God to move among the Christians in your nation, making the items on your Faith list (or activities like them) come true. Pray about how you or your group could be involved.

Continue to pray for the items on the list created in session 1.

Acting Out in Faith

After the prayer time, select one of the activities in the Faith column. Brainstorm how you or your group could initiate this activity. Whom could you contact? What resources do you have? What resources would you need to acquire? What could be your part in the development? Dare to dream big. Then be ready to go through the doors God might open.

A Passion for Peoples

If time allows, with the group or by yourself, complete a Hall of Fame chart for another nation that needs Christ at its center.

The next session: *Christ's mandate to make disciples of all nations*

Our Mission to Disciple the Nations

On April 6, 1994, a plane was shot out of the sky, killing the presidents of the African nations of Burundi and Rwanda. This attack sparked the beginning of a massive Rwandan genocide, in which 800,000 people were killed in four months.[7] Two million more became refugees beyond their borders. The brutality of the conflict between the Hutu and Tutsi tribes was unimaginable to people outside that country. People were killed one by one with spears and machetes. Neighbor killing neighbor. Today the name *Rwanda* is synonymous with genocide.

But there is another picture of Rwanda. Rwanda is a nation that has heard the gospel. Around the time of the genocide, most of Rwanda's people attended "Christian" churches.[8] So what happened? While many Rwandans had converted to Christianity, the central truths of Scripture hadn't resulted in a significant cultural transformation. Individuals accepted Jesus' claims, but in many cases their lives remained untransformed. Their society stayed unchanged as well.

During much of the twentieth century, the church has defined Christ's Great Commission in Matthew 28:18–20 as evangelism and conversion but not personal and national transformation. Bringing people to faith is an important task, but is this all Jesus meant when he asked his followers to "make disciples of all nations"?

In this session you'll learn that Christ's Great Commission is far more than a call to "win souls for Christ." It's a mandate to bring entire nations under the reign and authority of Jesus the King. It's a commission that aims at nothing less than the transformation and significant healing of entire nations.

KEY WORDS TO KNOW
An Order from the King

Commission

While this word has different meanings, this session uses the definition "a charge, order, or mandate." The Great Commission is Christ's order, or mandate, to his disciples. The proclamation is "great" because it was the Lord's final teaching, and it summarizes the church's role until he returns.

Disciple

The word *disciple* is derived from the Latin word *discipulus*, which means the "pupil" or "learner" of a teacher. In the Gospels, Jesus' associates were known as disciples, especially the twelve apostles. Yet the disciples' bond to the Master extended beyond a simple student-teacher relationship. Their discipleship to Jesus required personal allegiance and loyalty to him. They put Jesus first and applied his teaching to every area of their lives, regardless of the personal cost.

Christ's command to "make disciples" in the Great Commission calls the church to invite people from all nations to follow him.

Ordinance

An ordinance is a rule, statute, or decree established by someone in authority, such as a king or sovereign power. This session refers to God's or Christ's ordinances and decrees.

KEY VERSES TO READ

Making Disciples of All Nations

Then the eleven disciples went to Galilee, to the mountain where Jesus had told them to go. When they saw him, they worshipped him; but some doubted. Then Jesus came to them and said, "All authority in heaven and on earth has been given to me. Therefore go and make disciples of all nations, baptizing them in the name of the Father and of the Son and of the Holy Spirit, and teaching them to obey everything I have commanded you. And surely I am with you always, to the very end of the age."

—*Matthew 28:16–20*

1. What was "given" to the resurrected Christ?

2. In what realms does Christ reign? How far does his Lordship extend?

3. What does the word "therefore" refer to?

4. What is the primary task that Jesus gave his disciples?

5. Who will benefit from the completion of this task?

BIBLICAL INSIGHTS

Emissaries for Christ and Kingdom

After Christ's resurrection he reappeared to his disciples before ascending into heaven. On a sunny hillside overlooking the Sea of Galilee, he presented their final charge. Jesus Christ, the King of Heaven, commissioned them as his ambassadors. They would be his emissaries, establishing the "embassy" of the kingdom of God on earth. Since Christ rules through divine laws and ordinances, their task was to teach the nations to obey all that he commanded.

Jesus began the Great Commission by declaring His authority. "All authority in heaven and on earth has been given to me," he said. His claim was absolute. Even now, he declares himself the King of kings, who rules over creation from the right hand of God (Eph. 1:20–21; Heb. 10:12–13). He has conquered sin, death, and the devil. His claim of authority is both present (not future) and comprehensive (not limited). He *presently* exercises authority in every realm—physical, spiritual, social, cultural, educational, legal, political, and all other kinds of human endeavor. He is Lord of all!

Jesus' command followed: "Therefore, go." "Go" is a general calling for all believers. Some people have interpreted "go" as limited to professional missionaries called to witness for Jesus in other cultures, but this is a limited view of Christ's intention. Rather, the command to "go" is a call for all believers to make disciples, wherever they are. A more accurate translation of Christ's command is "as you are going." In essence Christ said, "As you are going, make disciples of all nations." It's a command for all who follow Christ: to make disciples in our families, neighborhoods, and communities, as well as in other countries and nations. It's a call to live totally devoted to God, in all we think, say, and do.

Reaching the Nations

Jesus commanded his disciples to go and "make disciples of all nations." His emphasis on "nations" is consistent with the emphasis on nations throughout the Bible. But what does it mean to make disciples of nations? Of course, nations are made up of individuals. Certainly, we're commanded to share the gospel with individuals, and if they put their faith in Jesus, we're to baptize and disciple them according to Christ's teachings. This is a common and correct understanding of this command, but it still misses something critical. Christ used the word "nations" as the object of this command, so what does this mean for us?

A nation is more than a group of individuals who share a common ethnicity and geographic location. In the Bible the English word *nation* is derived from the Latin *natio*, meaning birth, race, or nation, and is how we have translated the Greek word *ethnos*, which refers to a distinct ethnic or language group, and the Hebrew *goy*.

Members of a nation share both a common language and a set of values. This culture is manifested in its various realms or "spheres." These spheres include families, arts, sciences, media, law, government, education, and business. God is concerned with individuals and their corporate lives together as nations. He desires his rule and reign to impact every sphere of the societies in which we live. Why? Because all authority belongs to Jesus. He is Lord of all!

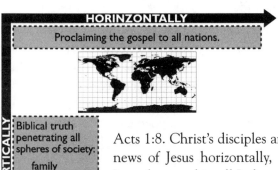

In fact, the command to make disciples of all nations has both a horizontal and vertical dimension. The horizontal dimension is reflected in Acts 1:8. Christ's disciples are to proclaim the good news of Jesus horizontally, to all the nations, "in Jerusalem, and in all Judea and Samaria, and to the ends of the earth." This is the grand task of frontier mission—proclaiming the gospel horizontally, to every "unreached" corner of the globe.

But there is a vertical dimension to the Great Commission as well. The church is to serve as "salt and light" (Matt. 5:13–19) within society. We are to live our everyday lives in such a way that truth, goodness and beauty penetrate vertically into every sphere of society: into our families, our neighborhoods, into the arts, science, commerce, education, and politics—every part—until entire cultures are transformed.

Considering that Christ is Lord of all, discipling the nations extends his rule and reign over all creation! His Great Commission aims at nothing short of the complete and total transformation of entire nations. This process begins as the Holy Spirit's power brings new birth to individuals. While personal salvation is the essential starting point in the process, it is not the end. The end arrives when God's perfect will and intentions are obeyed "on earth as [they are] in heaven" (Matt. 6:10), not just in individual lives but in every part of creation, in every sphere of society.

Even though this discipling process won't be completed until Jesus returns, we're commanded to work toward this goal until that day (Luke 19:11–13). In short, the church can't fulfill the command to "make disciples of all nations" solely by saving souls and starting new churches, but it can't fulfill the command without starting here, either.

The Secondary Commands

In addition to the primary command to "go and make disciples of all nations," there are two secondary instructions. They are "baptizing them in the name of the Father and of the Son and of the Holy Spirit" and "teaching them to obey everything I have commanded you."

The word *baptizing* is derived from the Greek word *baptizo*. A picture of *baptizo* appears in the work of the Greek poet and physician Nicander, who lived about 200 B.C. It's in his recipe for making pickles! (Pickles are vegetables that have been preserved and flavored in a solution of brine or vinegar.) According to Nicander, to make a pickle, a vegetable is first "dipped" (*bapto*) into boiling water, then "baptized" (*baptizo*) in a vinegar solution. Both verbs indicate immersing vegetables in a solution. The first (*bapto*) is temporary. The second, (*baptizo*, the act of baptizing the vegetable) produces a permanent change.

In the New Testament, *baptizo* (which produces permanent change) refers to our union and identification with Christ. In the Great Commission, Jesus said that simply believing the truth isn't enough. There must also be a union with him, resulting in a real change—like the vegetable to the pickle!

This transforming nature of baptism is often neglected. Just as Christ is God in human flesh, we as Christians (and our local churches) are called to reflect Jesus Christ in this broken world. When Christ's disciples live in a way that reflects the character of God, then the multiplied effect of their lives will profoundly impact the nations. Isn't that exciting?

The second instruction is to teach the nations to obey "all that I have commanded." God wants all nations transformed from their current brokenness into the glory of his good intentions. As presented in the last session, at the end of the age each nation will stand in God's presence, revealing its unique glory and splendor. This transformation occurs as Christ's commands are reflected in every sphere of its society. Since Jesus is God in human flesh, "all that I have commanded" encompasses all of God's recorded revelation through Scripture.

As increasing numbers of people in a nation believe in God and obey his commands, they'll be transformed spiritually and personally. As they live this transformation in every sphere of society, their nations will be transformed too. While no nation will be completely healed on this side of Christ's return, there exists the hope for substantial healing. Christ's message and power promise healing.

DISCOVERY QUESTIONS
Bringing Meaning to the Mission

The significance of the Great Commission holds even more meaning when you study the Scriptures yourself. Open your Bible to read more about God's plan for the nations and for you.

1. How is the reign and authority of Jesus described in these passages?

    Isaiah 9:7

    _____

    _____

Daniel 7:13–14

Ephesians 1:20–22

Philippians 2:9–11

Revelation 19:16

2. Read Colossians 1:15–18. What did Jesus create?

3. What is his present relationship with creation?

4. Over what does he have "supremacy"?

5. Colossians 1:18 concludes, "so that in everything he might have the supremacy." How does his supremacy over everything influence your understanding of Christ's command to "make disciples of all nations"? How broadly and deeply should this command extend?

_____

_____

_____

6. Jesus commands us to "make disciples." According to these passages, what does he mean by "disciple"?

    Mark 8: 34–35

    _____

    _____

    Mark 10:21, 28–29

    _____

    _____

    Luke 14:26–33

    _____

    _____

KEY POINTS TO REMEMBER
Embracing the Great Commission

1. Jesus rules over all creation, from the right hand of God.
2. The Great Commission calls us to bring entire nations under Christ's authority.
3. Christ's command "therefore go" tells believers to make disciples wherever they are, living in total devotion to God.
4. Personal salvation is the essential starting point for making disciples of all nations.
5. In the New Testament, "baptism" refers to our union and identification with Jesus—a union resulting in a real spiritual and personal change.
6. While no nation will be completely healed before Christ's return, there can be substantial healing.

CLOSING THOUGHTS
A Call to Faithfulness

Throughout Scripture, God expresses his love for all nations and his many promises to bless them. The Great Commission is a restatement of this theme, directed to the church. According to this commission, the church is to make disciples of all nations. The church is to overwhelm the nations with the majesty of the living God. The church is to bring the order of the kingdom of God to the nations. The church is to seek the blessing, healing, and restoration of all nations—not only at the end of the age but in the present one. God's kingdom will advance as the church models and speaks his nature, character, and commands.

God will faithfully carry out his purposes, and all nations will be blessed. This reality brings hope to each nation of the world. God also presents a clear challenge to the church in our day. Will we appreciate the full scope of his mandate and faithfully carry it out? Or will God wait for another faithful generation?

Remember: Being a disciple isn't easy, but with God all things are possible (Matt. 19:26).

PERSONAL APPLICATION
Planning for Everyday Change

Use these final questions to think about your understanding and relationship to the Great Commission. How can it affect you personally?

1. Before this session, what was your understanding of the Great Commission?

   _____

   _____

   _____

2. Has your understanding of Christ's mandate changed as a result of this session? If so, how?

---

3. Think about how this new understanding could change your every-day focus, activities, and attitudes. What changes, if any, do you need to make? What action could you take in your daily relationships?

---

4. Is there more life-changing action to take in the future? (For example, God could be calling you to make a career, location, lifestyle, or involvement change.) What might that be? How do you feel about this?

---

5. This week ask God to help you to make these changes, beginning with a small step. Write down what you intend to do. Share your decision with a friend who'll encourage you during the change process.

A PRACTICAL RESPONSE
Called and Commissioned

You've encountered lots of information in this study. Hopefully, it's inspired you to reach individuals and your nation for Christ. The following activities can provide closure to these sessions and motivate your commitment to the nations. While the instructions are worded for group leaders so that they can facilitate closure in a group setting, the collage activity can be completed by individuals as well.

A Commitment Collage

Before the last group meeting, the group leader can gather up old magazines, newspapers, and other publications that contain photos and illustrations. When the group reaches this part of the session, spread them out on a table or on the floor, accompanied with enough scissors, glue and/or tape, and large sheets of paper or poster board for each group member. From visuals and words in the publications, each participant can create a collage that represents his or her commitment to the nations. Participants can cut out images/words that represent their nations, their call to the Great Commission, the changes they need to make to follow this mandate, the feelings they harbor about this call and the personal changes it requires, and anything else that represents their involvement in the Great Commission, now or in the future.

Even though this activity sounds elementary, don't be reluctant to complete it. You'll be inspired by the insight and creativity that spring from the group. Ask group members to take their collages home and place them where they can see and be inspired by their artwork's meaning in the coming weeks.

Pray for Participants

Ask each person to explain his or her collage, and then pray for that individual's involvement in the Great Commission. Place a time limit on each person's explanation and group intercession so that every group member can be listened to and prayed for sufficiently. Designate someone to close in a final prayer, commissioning the group into the wonderful mission of discipling nations.

≈ Endnotes

1. Updated statistical information on global hunger can be accessed through The Hunger Project, 15 E. 26th Street, New York, NY 10010. www.thp.org.

2. In Genesis 12:1–3, the man is named Abram. God changed his name to Abraham (Gen. 17:5), indicating that he would be the father of many nations. In this study he is referred to as Abraham.

3. Thomas Cahill, *The Gifts of the Jews* (New York: Nan A. Talese, 1998), pp. 240–241.

4. Walter Wangerin, Jr. *Reliving the Passion* (Grand Rapids: Zondervan, 1992), p. 116.

5. Dan Allender and Tremper Longman III, *Bold Love* (Colorado Springs: NavPress, 1992), p. 78.

6. "Just and the Justifier," *Tabletalk*, published by Ligonier Ministries and R. C. Sproul, March 2002, p. 23.

7. Facts from the History Place on May 14, 2002. http://www.historyplace.com/index.html

8. Catholic 64.8%; Protestant 9.2%; Muslim 9%; tribal religions 17%. These 1995 statistics come from Organisation Internationale de la Francophonie on May 14, 2002. Cabinet du Secrétaire général de l'OIF, 28, rue de Bourgogne, 75007 Paris, France. http://www.francophonie.org/oif.cfm

⁓ Leader's Guide

We suggest the following guidelines for people leading study groups through this Bible study. Of course you will need to adapt the studies and our suggestions to your particular group and culture.

Preparing for and Facilitating a Group

◆ We suggest meeting for one hour per session. This will allow:

  ❖ 20 minutes to review the Key Verses and Biblical Insights sections.

  ❖ 20 minutes to discuss the Discovery Questions and Personal Application sections.

  ❖ 10 minutes to pray for one another.

  ❖ 10 minutes for general prayer and worship.

◆ To ensure that everyone contributes to the conversation, it's best to keep the group at six to eight participants (no more than twelve). If the membership increases, consider splitting into smaller groups during the discussion times and coming back together for concluding prayer.

◆ If group members have their own books, ask them to complete the session individually before they attend the meeting.

◆ To guide the group effectively, complete each session yourself before you meet together. Make sure you understand the main points of each session. Think about how they apply to your own life. Then, as you lead the group, you can better facilitate the discussion by clarifying the questions when needed and offering suggestions if the conversation lags.

◆ For each session, before you meet together, read through the Practical Response ideas at the end of the lesson. If you plan to complete one or more of the activities as a group, bring any necessary supplies to the meeting.

◆ For each meeting, arrive ahead of time to prepare the location (chairs, refreshments, teaching aids, etc.) and to greet group members as they arrive.

◆ For your first meeting, be sure to take time to introduce each group member. You may wish to do an activity that will help group members get to know each other. Introduce the study by presenting key ideas from the Introduction and reading the overall objectives for the sessions (listed in the Study Notes following this Leader's Guide).

◆ Be a *facilitator*, not a teacher. Here are some suggestions:

❖ Encourage group participation. Sitting in a circle (rather than rows) can help.

❖ Use group members' names.

❖ Ask different people to pray and read.

❖ Ask questions and wait for answers. Don't immediately give your own answer.

❖ Thank group members for their ideas, and ask others what they think.

❖ Draw out members who aren't contributing much.

❖ Tactfully redirect the focus from participants who tend to dominate the discussion.

❖ Ask participants for explanation when they give simple "yes" or "no" answers.

❖ Pace your study at a rate that allows for group members' maximum understanding. Review as often as necessary.

❖ Keep the session objective in mind as you work through the session. These objectives, as well as possible responses for questions, are listed in the Study Notes.

Suggestions for Leading Each Session

◆ Have a group member open and close each meeting time with prayer.

◆ Begin the meeting by reviewing the Key Points to Remember from the previous session. Take time to discuss how group members may have applied the teaching from the previous session since the last meeting.

◆ You may wish to assign the Key Verses to Read as a memorization exercise. If so, take time at the beginning of the session to allow group members to recite the verses corresponding to the session. This can easily be done in pairs to save time.

- ◆ Refer back to the Key Words to Know section as necessary during discussion.
- ◆ Read the Key Verses to Read and answer the questions provided as a group. (See possible responses to these questions in the Study Notes.)
- ◆ If each group member has a book, take turns reading the Biblical Insights section together. If you're the only one with a book, share the main points or read this section to the group. The Key Points to Remember section will help present the main ideas.
- ◆ Answer the Discovery Questions together as a group. (See possible responses to these questions in the Study Notes.)
- ◆ Answer the Personal Application questions together as a group. If group members have their own books, you may wish to break up into smaller groups (two to three people) and have each subgroup read and answer the Personal Application questions.
- ◆ Work on a Practical Response activity if you've chosen to do so. These optional ideas are provided to help group members apply the session's main points in their own lives.
- ◆ You will find the session Objectives, Possible Responses to Questions for Key Verses to Read, and Possible Responses to Discovery Questions for each session in the Study Notes that follow this Leader's Guide.

Study Notes

Whether you lead or participate in a small group or study alone, you may find it helpful to consult the session objectives and suggested responses for each session's Biblical Insights and Discovery questions. Not all questions have a "right" or "wrong" answer, but these suggestions will help stimulate your thinking.

Session 1: God's Remarkable Plan for the Nations

Objective: To describe the nature of God's redemptive plan and how it has unfolded through the centuries.

Possible Responses to Questions for Key Verses to Read

1. His country, his people, and his father's household
2. "to the land I will show you"
3. "Go to the land I will show you." "I will make you into a great nation." "I will bless you." "I will make your name great." "I will bless those who bless you." "I will curse those who curse you."
4. All the nations on earth will be blessed.
5. To bless every nation on earth

Possible Responses to Discovery Questions

1a. He determined the times set for each nation, as well as their exact geographic location.
1b. God desires for all nations to seek and reach out to him.
1c. God created all nations. They can trace their lineage back to Adam and Eve.
2a. To make the "unchanging nature of his purpose very clear to the heirs of what was promised"
2b. God's oath assures us that he will bless his children and all nations.
2c. God's oath gives assurance to every nation—even the poorest and most downcast—that he will bless them.

3. Each passage shows God's promise to Abraham being fulfilled as the nations of the world acknowledge the Creator and worship him.
4. It could bring hope, healing, joy, and blessing to our nation.

Session 2: Israel's Important Role in God's Plan

Objective: To describe how God worked through Abraham's offspring—the nation of Israel—to carry out the first stage of his redemptive plan.

Possible Responses to Questions for Key Verses to Read

1. That God's ways may be known on the earth through Israel
2. He desires "all the peoples" to praise him, to be glad and sing for joy. He desires the "ends of the earth" to revere him.
3. He is described as the one who rules "the peoples" justly and guides the nations of the earth.
4. The land will yield its harvest. God will bless Israel, and all nations will revere him.
5. Both speak of God's promise to bless Abraham's offspring (Israel) and to bless the nations of the world through Israel.

Possible Responses to Discovery Questions

1. He chose Israel because he loved them (set his affection on them) and swore an oath to Abraham, the forefather of Israel, to bless his offspring. He did not choose them because they had more people than other nations.
2. From their slavery and oppression in Egypt
3. To walk in his ways, and to obey (follow) his laws and decrees
4. It will "go well" for Israel, now and in the future. They will "live long" in the land God is giving them. God will reveal his wisdom, understanding, and power to other nations through them.
5. They will learn that Israel is a wise, blessed nation. They will learn that God exists, that he desires obedience, and that obedience has practical benefits.
6. God's revealed truth was given to Israel, and then spread around the world. It has impacted our nation and has penetrated the culture,

influencing our values, view of human life, and the way our nation is ordered.

Session 3: Jesus, the Center of God's Plan

Objective: To describe why Jesus is the centerpiece of God's redemptive plan and what was accomplished through his sacrificial death and resurrection.

Possible Responses to Questions for Key Verses to Read

1. The fullness of God is in Jesus.
2. To reconcile all things to God
3. Things on earth and things in heaven
4. Through Christ's blood shed on the cross

Possible Responses to Discovery Questions

1. A sinful person cannot please God.
2. Everyone is a sinner.
3. God's judgment, wrath, and anger—and ultimately death
4. He saved us and "made us alive."
5. *Romans 8:1–4:* There is no condemnation. We've been set free from sin and death. The righteous requirements of the law are fully met in us. Christ's righteousness has been imputed to us.
   2 Corinthians 5:21: We now have the righteousness of God.
   Ephesians 1:7: We have been redeemed, and our sins, forgiven.
   Revelation 1:5–6: We have freedom from sin. We've been made into a kingdom of priests to serve God.
6. *2 Corinthians 5:17–19:* We are a "new creation."
   Ephesians 2:4–7: We are "made alive" and raised up with Christ and seated in the heavenly realms.
7. The old covenant was between God and Israel. It required their complete obedience to God's law. If they violated God's laws and decrees, animal sacrifices were required to make atonement for their sins. Such sacrifices had to be offered over and over again.

   The new covenant is between God and people from all nations who have put their faith in the saving work of Jesus and live lives of obedience to him. Unlike the animal sacrifices of the old covenant, Christ's sacrificial death on the cross atones for their sins once and for all.

Under the old covenant, the law was written on tablets of stone. Under the new covenant, the Holy Spirit comes to indwell followers of Jesus, and God's law is "written on their hearts" as opposed to the stone tablets of the old covenant.

The new covenant was necessary because the animal sacrifices could never truly atone for sins or restore a person into a right relationship with God. They served to only foreshadow Christ's perfect sacrifice on the cross for the sins of humankind.

8. Individuals' answers will vary.

Session 4: God's Purpose for the Church

Objective: To describe how and why God raised up the church to be his principle agent for advancing his redemptive plan in the present age.

Possible Responses to Questions for Key Verses to Read

1. In Exodus 19:5–6, God refers to Israel as "my treasured possession" and "a kingdom of priests and a holy nation." In 1 Peter 2:9–10, God (through the apostle Peter) calls the church "a people belonging to God" and "a royal priesthood, a holy nation."
2. It is significant because prior to Jesus, the only people referred to as "the people of God" were those from the nation of Israel.
3. So they could "declare the praises" of God to the rest of the world
4. Israel was blessed by God to make him known to the nations of the world. The same is now true of the church.

Possible Responses to Discovery Questions

1. Through "the blood of Christ" and placing "faith in Christ"
2. In Exodus 19:6, it's Israel. In Revelation 5:9–10, it's the worldwide church.
3. The church must see itself as "the body of Jesus" in the midst of the unbelieving world. It represents Christ and reflects him to the world.

It can share the gospel and work to bring hope and healing in the name of Jesus.

4. *John 10:14–16:* God's sheep
   Galatians 6:16: the Israel of God
   Ephesians 1:22–23: the body of Christ
   Ephesians 2:19–22: fellow citizens with God's people and members of God's household
   Ephesians 3:15: the family of God
   1 Peter 2:9: God's chosen people, a royal priesthood, a holy nation, a people belonging to God
   Revelation 19:7: the bride of Christ

5. The source of unity is our common relationship with God and the same Holy Spirit who lives within us all. Our diversity is in different gifts, services, and "offices" or functions.

6. As Christ's "body" here on earth, the church is to reflect the fullness of Jesus before the watching eyes of the world.

Session 5: The Glory of the Nations

Objective: To describe the blessings that God holds in store for the nations when he returns to earth at the end of the age.

Possible Responses to Questions for Key Verses to Read

1. A great multitude from every nation, tribe, people, and language
2. *Isaiah 1:18:* The white robes represent the washing away of sins.
   Revelation 19:6–8: The white robes represent the righteous acts of the saints.
3. The Lamb. God. The Alpha and the Omega. He is the Lamb because he is the final, perfect sacrifice, atoning for the sins of humanity. He is God, the sovereign Creator and Ruler. He is the Alpha and the Omega, the beginning and end of everything.
4. There will be no more hunger, thirst, sorrow, sadness, or death. Jesus will guide the nations and "lead them to springs of living water."

Possible Responses to Discovery Questions

1. People from all nations
2. They will be worshiping God and singing praises to him.
3. The nations will be glad and sing for joy. They will worship God.
4. The "wealth and riches" and the "glory and honor" of the nations

Session 6: Our Mission to Disciple the Nations

Objective: To explain why the Great Commission (Matt. 28:18–20) is far more than a call to "win souls for heaven"; it is a mandate to bring entire nations under the reign and authority of Jesus the King.

Possible Responses to Questions for Key Verses to Read

1. All authority in heaven and on earth
2. He reigns in all realms. His Lordship extends over all creation.
3. The fact that Christ has all authority over all creation
4. To make disciples of all nations
5. All nations

Possible Responses to Discovery Questions

1. Jesus' reign and authority is never ending. His kingdom will never be destroyed. His authority is "far above all rule and authority, power, and dominion and every title that can be given" (Eph. 1:20–22). Everyone will confess to his Lordship. He is the "King of kings and Lord of lords" (Rev. 19:16).
2. He created "all things."
3. In him, "all things hold together." He sustains all things moment by moment.
4. He has supremacy over "all things."
5. His command to make disciples of all nations should extend to "all things," and not just to human souls. His Lordship is over everything, so everything should be impacted.
6. Jesus' understanding of a disciple is someone who is willing to give up everything to follow him.

About the Authors

Darrow L. Miller is a vice president with Food for the Hungry International and cofounder of the Disciple Nations Alliance. He has served with FHI since 1981. His passion is helping people understand and apply the biblical worldview so that nations can be released from hunger and poverty. His book *Discipling Nations* (1998, YWAM Publishing) reveals his heart to renew the church's vision for discipling nations. Darrow has an M.A. in adult education. He has four grown children and lives with his wife, Marilyn, in Cave Creek, Arizona.

Bob Moffitt is president of the Harvest Foundation and co-founder of the Disciple Nations Alliance. For over thirty years he has developed and directed Christian organizations designed to encourage and enable Christians to demonstrate God's love, especially to broken people and their communities. He writes and teaches curricula designed to enable lay Christians to live out their faith in practical terms, particularly in the context of their local churches. He and his wife, Judy, live in Phoenix, Arizona.

Scott D. Allen is the worldwide coordinator of the Disciple Nations Alliance. He has served with Food for the Hungry International (FHI) since 1989, serving as Director of Human Resource Development. He has also served as a missionary in Japan, teaching English through local churches in the Osaka area. Scott has a bachelor's degree in history and education from Willamette University in Salem, Oregon. Scott lives with his wife, Kim, and their four children in Phoenix, Arizona.

Other KINGDOM LIFESTYLE Bible Studies

Revolutionizing Lives and Renewing Minds!

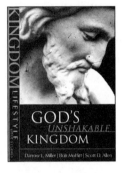

God's Unshakable Kingdom
by Scott D. Allen, Darrow L. Miller, and Bob Moffitt

The concept of the kingdom of God is one of the most confusing and misunderstood ideas in the Bible. Yet it's indisputable that the kingdom of God was central to Jesus' teachings. As he ministered, Jesus talked passionately about the kingdom. The phrase "kingdom of God" or "kingdom of heaven" appears ninety-eight times in the New Testament, more than sixty times on the lips of Jesus. This profound study explores the kingdom of God, helping believers build a biblical understanding of the vision for which Jesus lived and died—a vision that transforms individuals, families, churches, and whole nations.

ISBN 1-57658-346-5

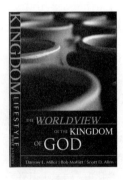

The Worldview of the Kingdom of God
by Scott D. Allen, Darrow L. Miller, and Bob Moffitt

Today, there are more churches and more Christians in the world than at any time in history. But to what end? Poverty and corruption thrive in developing countries that have been evangelized. Moral and spiritual poverty reign in the "Christian" West. Why? Because believers don't have the "mind of Christ." All of us have a worldview, or a mental model of the world. This set of ideas and assumptions ultimately determines the choices we make and the kind of lives we lead. *The Worldview of the Kingdom of God* explores the biblical worldview and why understanding it and living it out are essential to leading a fruitful, abundant life.

ISBN 1-57658-351-1

Disciple
Nations
Alliance

Founded by:
Harvest and Food for
the Hungry International

The Disciple Nations Alliance (DNA) is a global movement of individuals, churches, and organizations with a common vision: to see engaged, credible, high-impact local churches effecting real transformation in their communities and in sufficient mass to disciple their nations.

DNA was founded in 1997 through a partnership between Food for the Hungry and Harvest. Our mission is to envision churches with a biblical worldview and equip them to practice a wholistic, incarnational ministry affecting all spheres of society. We provide simple tools that enable churches to begin the transformation process immediately with existing resources—no matter how materially poor they may be.

If you would like more information about the Disciple Nations Alliance or our teaching and training resources, please visit our website: www.disciplenations.org.

Disciple Nations Alliance

1220 E. Washington Street
Phoenix, Arizona 85034
www.disciplenations.org

Founding Partners

Food for the Hungry International
www.fhi.net

Harvest Foundation
www.harvestfoundation.org

Samaritan Strategy Africa

The messages and teaching contained in the Kingdom Lifestyle Bible Studies are being championed throughout the continent of Africa through the efforts of Samaritan Strategy Africa, a collaborative network of African churches and Christian organizations that have banded together to accomplish the urgent goal of awakening, equipping, and mobilizing the African church to rise up and transform society. Through training, mentoring, conferences, and publications, Samaritan Strategy Africa aims to help churches

- ◆ discover God's vision of comprehensive healing and transformation of the nations;
- ◆ adopt a biblical worldview and then live it out by taking truth, goodness, and beauty into every sphere of society;
- ◆ practice a ministry of outreach within the community, demonstrating Christ's love to needy and broken people through works of service.

If you would like more information about Samaritan Strategy Africa or you would like to find out about upcoming training events or how you, your church, or your organization can be involved, we invite you to visit our website or contact us.

Samaritan Strategy Africa

Dennis Tongoi, Team Leader
PO Box 40360, 00100
Nairobi, Kenya
Phone: (254) 20-2720037/56
Email: afg@cms-africa.org
Website: www.samaritan-strategy-africa.org

Samaritan Strategy Africa is affiliated with the Disciple Nations Alliance (DNA), a global movement founded in 1997 through a partnership between Food for the Hungry and Harvest. DNA exists to see engaged, credible, high-impact local churches effecting real transformation in their communities and in sufficient mass to disciple their nations. For more information, visit www.disciplenations.org.